Life on the Edge

D0047649

Life on the Edge

DR JAMES DOBSON

WORD
BOOKS

WORD PUBLISHING
Nelson Word Ltd
Milton Keynes, England

WORD AUSTRALIA
Kilsyth, Australia

STRUIK CHRISTIAN BOOKS (PTY) LTD
Cape Town, South Africa

JOINT DISTRIBUTORS SINGAPORE–
ALBY COMMERCIAL ENTERPRISES LTD
and
CAMPUS CRUSADE ASIA LTD

PHILIPPINE CAMPUS CRUSADE FOR CHRIST
Quezon City, Philippines

CHRISTIAN MARKETING NEW ZEALAND LTD
Havelock North, New Zealand

JENSCO LTD
Hong Kong

SALVATION BOOK CENTRE
Malaysia

LIFE ON THE EDGE

DEDICATION

*This book is dedicated to those for whom it was written
. . . the generation of young people currently moving out
of adolescence and into the arena of adult responsibility.
In a blink of an eye, they will inherit the businesses,
institutions and governments of the world. On their
shoulders will soon rest the burdens of leadership and
authority. They will pull the wagonload of humanity
behind them as their families emerge and grow. It is to
these bright and resourceful young adults that I devote
the pages of this book. With it comes a prayer that they
will remember and honour the heritag of faith handed
down to them by previous generations and then be
diligent to teach it to their children. There is no more
noble objective in living.*

CONTENTS

1

BLAST OFF
OR BLOW UP?

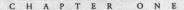

If you are between sixteen and twenty-six years of age, this book is written specifically for you. Others are welcome to read along with us, of course, but the ideas are aimed directly at those moving through what we will call the 'critical decade'.

Some of the most dramatic and permanent changes in life usually occur during these ten short years. A person is transformed from a kid who's still living at home and eating at the parents' table, to a fully-fledged adult who should be earning a living and taking complete charge of their own life. Most of the decisions that will shape the next fifty years will be made in this era, including the choice of an occupation, perhaps the decision to marry, and the establishment of values and principles by which life will be governed.

What makes this period even more significant is the impact of early mistakes and errors in judgement. They can undermine all that is to follow. A bricklayer knows he must be very careful to get his foundation absolutely straight; any unevenness in the bricks at the bottom will create an even greater tilt as the wall goes up. So it is in life.

This momentous journey through the critical decade reminds me of a trip our family took to Kenya and Tanzania a few years ago. The highlight of our tour was a visit to the Serengeti, a magnificent national park where legendary African animals roam wild and free. It had rained all day before we arrived, and the unpaved roads were extremely muddy. Before we had driven fifteen miles into the park, our car slid into a ditch and became bogged down to its axles in thick, African mud. We would have certainly spent the night out there on the savanna if it had not been for a native in a double-wheeled truck who gave us a hand.

Early mistakes and errors in judgement . . . can undermine all that is to follow.

Later that afternoon we came to a stretch of road that was even more torn up and muddy. There it divided and ran parallel for several hundred yards before merging back together. It was obvious that drivers earlier that day had forged a new trail to get around a mudhole, but we had no way of knowing on which side it lay. We sat there for a moment trying to decide which road to take. If we made a mistake, we would probably get stuck again and have to sleep in the car—without dinner, toothbrushes, bathroom facilities, or even water to drink.

Our seventeen-year-old son, Ryan, then volunteered to help.

'I'll run ahead and look at the road,' he said. 'Then I'll wave to let you know which way to go.'

The missionary who was with us said, 'Uhm, Ryan, I don't think that is a very good idea. You just don't know what might be out there in the tall grass.'

Eventually we chose what looked like the best road and were indeed able to get through. But when we reached the place where the two trails came back together, a surprise was waiting for us. A huge male lion was crouched in the grass off to one side. He rolled his big yellow eyes towards us and dared us to take him on. Large cats like that consider humans to be just another easy dinner. They can cover one hundred yards in less than three seconds and wouldn't hesitate to devour any city dweller who was foolish enough to tempt them.

Ryan looked at the lion and agreed that he probably ought to stay in the car!

BUT WHAT ABOUT THOSE MUDHOLES?

In a manner of speaking, our experience on the Serengeti illustrates the passage from late adolescence to young adulthood. The journey goes smoothly and uneventfully for some individuals. They drive right through without a hitch. But a surprisingly large number of us encounter unexpected 'mudholes' that trap and hold us at an immature stage of development. Others still are plagued by predators lurking in the tall grass. Among them are addiction to alcohol or drugs, marriage to the wrong person, failure to achieve a coveted dream, suicide, homicide, or various criminal offences. It is *very* easy to get off the trail and into the ditch in the morning of our lives.

Permit me another illustration that comes to mind. I was invited a few years ago to take a three-day whitewater rafting trip down the Rogue River in Oregon. A friend and experienced rafter, Dr Richard Hosley, said to me as we were preparing to launch, 'One thing you'll soon learn is that the river is always boss.' I didn't know what he meant then, but three days later I understood that principle very clearly.

> *It is very easy to get off the trail and into the ditch in the morning of our lives.*

Rather than floating on the raft for fifty miles in relative serenity and safety, I chose to paddle along behind in a plastic eight-foot canoe. And on the second afternoon, I insisted on rowing this flimsy craft into the most treacherous part of the river. It was a bad decision.

Ahead lay a section of the river known as the 'Coffeepot', so named because the narrowing of the rock-walled banks create an unpredictable, bubbling current that has been known to suck small boats and their passengers below the surface without warning. Several men and women have drowned in that precise spot, one of them only the summer before. But ignorance is bliss, and blissful I was.

I seemed to be handling the task quite well for the first few minutes . . . before everything became unglued. I was then caught in the current flowing around a large rock and capsized in the turbulent water. It seemed like an eternity before I came to the surface, only to find breathing impossible. A bandanna that had been around my neck was now plastered across my mouth and held there by my glas-ses, which were strapped to my head. Just as I clawed free and gasped for air, churning water hit me in the face and gurgled into my lungs. Again, I came up coughing and spluttering before taking another trip below the surface. By then I was desperate for air and keenly aware that the Coffeepot was only a hundred yards downstream.

A kind of panic gripped me that I had not experienced since childhood! I definitely considered the possibility that I was drowning. You see, I have a nagging little habit of breathing every few minutes and do not cope well when prevented from doing so. I knew that getting sucked under again at that moment might be the end of the line. My family and friends watched helplessly from the raft as I bobbed through the rapids and into the narrowest section of the river. They were unable to reach me because the current had carried them further downstream.

By using his incredible rafting skill, however, Dr Hosley managed to 'hold' the raft by manoeuvring it to an eddy at the side of the river. There it spun until I caught up and grabbed the rope that rims the upper exterior structure. I could not pull myself onto the raft because of the rapids, my soaked clothing, and the distance of the rope above my head. That's why I expected Dr Hosley to help me aboard. Instead, I noticed that he was struggling with the oars and looking very concerned. I learned later what was worrying him. He feared that the large raft would be thrown against the vertical rock walls bordering the Coffeepot and that I would be crushed by its massive force.

No one travels down the river of life without encountering turbulence.

Indeed, the raft *was* thrown against the wall, but I saw it coming. Using all of the strength left within me, I pulled my feet up and sprang off the rock, propelling myself high enough onto the raft to scramble on board. I then collapsed in the bottom and stayed there sucking in air for about thirty minutes.

The only casualty from the experience is a matter of collegiate pride. Dr Hosley was wearing a shirt with the name of his beloved Stanford University across the front. It survived the trip. But somewhere on the bottom of the Rogue River in dishonour lies a waterlogged hat bearing the logo of the University of Southern California. It was a sad moment in the historic rivalry of the two schools. At least I didn't wind up lying on the rocky bottom clutching my USC banner!

You can probably see how this story relates to our theme. Life is like the beautiful Rogue River in some ways. There are long stretches when the water is calm and serene. You can see your reflection as you lean out of the raft. The scenery is gorgeous, and the river carries you peacefully downstream. Then without warning you are propelled into the white water. Suddenly, you're gasping for air and struggling to keep your head above water. At the moment when you think you might be drowning, you float right into the turmoil of the Coffeepot.

Please understand that this **will** happen to you sooner or later. No one travels down the river of life without encountering turbulence. You might as well brace yourself for it. There will be moments of serenity and beauty when you lean back and take in the wonder. But there will also be times of sheer terror when you'll be tossed out of the boat and at the mercy of the good Lord. It's all part of the ride. That's why it is necessary before these crises arrive to get yourself stabilised—to figure out who you are and what you will do when the pressure is on.

THEY CALL IT THE 'CRITICAL DECADE'

Your next ten years will pose hundreds of important questions for which secure answers may be slow in coming. I struggled with many of them when I was in college, such as, What will I do with my life? What kind of woman should I marry? Where will I find her? Will our love last a lifetime? What are my strengths and weaknesses? Should I plan to attend graduate school? Can I qualify for admission? Am I talented enough to make it professionally? And what about God? Where does He fit into my plans, and how can I know His will? I recall pondering these questions and thinking how helpful it would be to talk with someone who had a few answers—someone who understood what I was facing. But like most of my friends, I never asked for help. The years rolled on, and I gradually bobbed and weaved my way through the 'white water'.

Of course, it was easier to go it alone when I was young. The river was less turbulent in those years. I grew up in the 'Happy Days' of the fifties, when life was not as complicated. There were no drugs in my racially mixed, state high school. Can you believe it? Not once did I hear of anyone selling or using illegal substances while I was a student there.

And very little alcohol was consumed by today's standards. None of my friends made a habit of drinking. In fact, I went to parties every Friday night after football games and rarely saw 'booze' being consumed. It happened, I'm sure, but primarily among those who had a reputation for being on the 'wild side'. There were no punkers, no skinheads, no neo-Nazis, no freaks, no witches, and no gay or lesbian activists in those days. And the music of that era was pretty tame by comparison.

No doubt, some of my classmates lost their virginity during their school years. Sex is not a recent discovery, and it was certainly on our minds in those bygone days. Obviously, some students did more than think about it. Every now and then a girl became pregnant (then it was called being 'in trouble') and was immediately packed off to some secret location. I never knew where they went. Still, the idea of saving oneself for marriage made a lot of sense. Morality was fashionable. Students who slept around were disrespected by their peers. Promiscuous girls were called 'sluts', and promiscuous boys were said to be 'on the make'. Couples living together out of wedlock were 'living in sin' or 'shacking up'. It

Our culture has gone into a kind of moral free fall.

never occurred to us that virginity was a curse to be got rid of or that adults expected us to copulate like animals on heat. That wicked notion would come along in the modern era, when everyone from the school nurse to a misguided Chief Medical Officer seemed to be chanting, 'Do it often. Do it right. Use a condom every night'.

Finally, and most importantly, students in the fifties were often receptive to spiritual influences. They were not all Christians of course, but many of us were. Our faith shaped the way we behaved, too. For example, God's name was rarely used profanely. The punctuation of speech with vulgarity and irreverence did not become fashionable for most teenagers until the late sixties, when it was popularised by decadent film and television industries. They also taught many members of your parents' generation to engage in casual sex and to disregard the commandments of God. Many revolutionary changes occurred during the late sixties when that generation of young adults suddenly went a little crazy. They've paid a high price for it, too.

My point is that the world in which you live has become much more immoral than it was just a few decades ago. It is not uncommon now for twelve-year-olds to have babies and fifteen-year-olds to shoot each other and seventeen-year-olds to be addicted to hard drugs and eighteen-year-olds to be infected with the AIDS virus. And where violence has become a way of life—especially for kids living in the inner city. A child in the United States was fifteen times more likely to be killed by gunfire[1] than a kid growing up in Northern Ireland, which had a long history of violence, before the inauguration of the peace process. Some children have to sleep in bathtubs at night just to be protected from drive-by shootings. Yes, our culture has gone into a kind of moral free fall that has implications for everyone who is young. Consequently, we are forced to deal with pressures and temptations that previous generations did not have to face.

One of the most important decisions to be made in the next few years will focus on a life's work—an occupation—or a skill you hope to develop. That choice is often extremely difficult. How can you predict what you'll want to be doing when you're forty or fifty or sixty years of age? You're obligated to guess, based on very limited information. You may not even know what the work is really like, yet you enrol yourself in a lengthy academic programme to train for it.

The decisions you make under those circumstances may

lock you into something you will later hate. And there are social pressures that influence your choices. For example, many young women secretly want to be wives and mothers, but are afraid to admit it in today's 'liberated' society. Furthermore, how can a girl plan to do something that requires the participation of another person—a husband who will be worthy of loving her and living with her for the rest of her life? Marriage may or may not be in the picture for her. Yes, there's plenty to consider in the critical decade.

I feel very fortunate to have stumbled into a profession when I was young that I have been able to do reasonably well. If I had been born in Jesus' time and had been required to earn a living with my hands, perhaps in carpentry or stonemasonry, I would have probably starved to death. I can see myself sitting outside the temple in Jerusalem with a sign that read, 'Will work for food'. Craftsmanship is just not in my nature. I earned my only high school 'D' in woodworking class, and that was a gift from my teacher, Mr Peterson. I spent an entire term trying to make a box in which to store shoe polish and brushes. What a waste! At least that experience helped me rule out a few occupational possibilities. Carpentry and cabinet-making were two of them.

THINGS TO CONSIDER WHEN CHOOSING A PROFESSION

You'll have to rule some things in and out, too. Indeed, to make an informed decision about a profession, you'll need to get six essential components together, as follows:

1. It must be something you genuinely like to do. This choice requires you to identify your own strengths, weaknesses and interests. (Some excellent psychometric tests are available to help with this need.)

2. It must be something you have the ability to do. You might want to be an attorney but lack the talent to do the academic work and pass the bar examination.

3. It must be something you can earn a living by. You might want to be an artist, but if people don't buy your paintings, you could starve while sitting at your easel.

4. It must be something you are permitted to do. You might make a wonderful physician and could handle the training but can't gain entrance to medical school. I went through a Ph.D. programme in graduate school with a fellow student who was washed out after seven years of classwork. He made it to the last major exam before his professors told him, 'You're out.'

5. It must be something that brings cultural affirmation. In other words, most people need to feel some measure of respect from their contemporaries for what they do. This is one reason why women have found it difficult to stay at home and raise their children.

6. Most important for the genuine believer, is it must be something that you feel God approves of. How do you determine the will of God about so personal a decision? That is a critical matter we'll discuss presently.

What makes it so tough to choose an occupation is that all six of these requirements must be met at the same time. If you get five of them down but you don't like what you have selected, you're in trouble. If you get five together but are rejected by the required professional schools, you are blocked. If you get five lined up but you can't earn a living at the job of your choice, the system fails. Every link in the chain must connect.

So many young people flounder during the critical decade.

Given this challenge, it isn't surprising that so many young people flounder during the critical decade. They become immobilised for years not knowing what to do next. They sit around their parents' house plunking on a guitar and waiting for a dish to rattle in the kitchen.

Young adults in this situation remind me of rockets sitting on the launch pad. Their engines are roaring and belching smoke and fire, but nothing moves. The spacecraft was made to blast its way through the stratosphere, but there it sits as if bolted to the pad. I've met many men and women in their early twenties whose rockets just would not lift them off the ground. And yes, I've known a few whose engines blew up and scattered the debris of broken dreams all over the launch pad.

The mission sometimes fails because an individual refuses to include God in his lofty plans. The psalmist wrote, 'Except the Lord build the house, they labour in vain that build it: except the LORD keep the city, the watchman waketh but in vain' (Psalm 127:1 KJV). Those words offer incredible meaning for those of you who are just getting started in life. Whatever you try to do, whether it is to build or defend, will be useless if you do it in your own strength. That may sound very old fashioned, but I promise you it is true. Furthermore, the Lord will not settle for second place in your life.

LESSONS FROM MY FATHER

My father thought he would be an exception to that principle. He had his life laid out, and he needed no help from God or anyone else in fulfilling it. From his early childhood, Dad knew he wanted to be a great artist. Even before kindergarten, he told his family he intended to draw and paint when he grew up. This passion was not simply a choice he had made. It was in his blood. All through child-hood and his teens, he never wavered from this desire to become another Rembrandt or Michelangelo. While his five brothers were uncertain about what they wanted to be, this youngest among them was chasing a lofty dream.

The Lord will not settle for second place in your life.

Then one day as he walked along a street during his sixteenth year, he seemed to hear the Lord speaking to him. It was not an audible voice, of course. But deep within his being he knew he had been addressed by the Almighty. It was a simple message that conveyed this thought: *I want you to set aside your great ambition to be an artist and prepare for a life of service in the ministry.*

My father was terrified by the experience. He replied, 'No! No, Lord. You know I have my plans all made and art is my consuming interest.' He quickly argued down the impression and convinced himself that his mind had deceived him. But when he got it all resolved and laid to rest, it would reappear. Month after month, the nagging thought reverberated in his mind that God was asking—no, demanding—that he abandon his dream and become a preacher. It proved to be one of the greatest struggles of his life, but he shared it with no one.

For two years this inner battle went on. Then towards the end of his senior year in high school, the time came for him to select a college to attend in the autumn. His father told him to pick out any school in the country and he would send him there. But what was he to do? If he yielded to the voice within, he would have to attend a college that would begin preparing him for the ministry. But if he followed his dream, he would go to art school. Would he obey God, or would he have his own way? It was a terrible dilemma.

One morning a few weeks before graduation, he got out

of bed to prepare for school. But the minute his feet touched the floor, my father heard the voice again. It was as if the Lord said, *Today you will have to make up your mind.* He wrestled with this issue all day at school but still shared his turmoil with no one. After his last class in midafternoon, he came home to an empty house. He paced back and forth in the living room, praying and struggling with this unrelenting demand of God. Finally, in an act of defiance, he suddenly turned his face upwards and said, 'It's too great a price, and I won't pay it!'

My father later described that moment as the most terrible experience of his life. He said the Spirit of the Lord seemed to leave him as one person would walk away from another. He was still shaken and pale when his mother came home a few minutes later. She could see his distress, and she asked him what was wrong.

'You won't understand this, Mum' he said, 'but God has been asking me to give up my plans to be an artist. He wants me to become a minister. I don't want to do it. And I won't do it. I've just said no to Him, and He's gone.'

My grandmother was a very righteous woman who could always touch the heart of God in her prayers. She said, 'Oh, Honey, you're just emotional. Let's pray about it.'

Would he obey God, or would he have his own way?

They got down on their knees, and my grandmother began talking to the Lord about her son. Then she stopped in midsentence. 'I don't understand it,' she said. 'Something is wrong.'

'You don't understand it,' said my father, 'but I do. I've just refused to obey God, and He's gone.'

It would be seven long years before my father would hear the voice of the Lord again. You see, his love of art had become his god. It mattered more to him than anything on earth and even outranked his relationship with the Father. That's what was going on in his heart. There was nothing sinful or immoral in his love of art. The problem was that God had no place in it.

In the next few days, my father chose the Art Institute of Pittsburgh (AIP), one of the best art schools in the country. He enrolled there in the autumn, and his professors immediately recognised his unusual talent. Indeed, when he graduated, he was honoured as the most gifted student in his class. But as he was walking down the aisle to the platform where a big 'Number One' banner had been draped on his paintings, the scripture again came into his mind: *Except the Lord build the house, they labour in vain that build it.*

My father graduated and went out to begin his great career in the field of art. Unfortunately, the Great Depression was underway in the United States and in most countries around the world. That was a scary time in American history when huge numbers of people were out of work. Businesses failed, banks closed, and opportunities were few and far between. My dad was one of the millions who couldn't find a job of any type—much less one in his chosen profession. He was finally hired at a Texaco service station to serve petrol and wipe the windscreens of cars. It was pretty humbling for a man who wanted to be another Leonardo da Vinci.

Here is the most incredible part of the story. Right at that moment when my dad was desperate for a career opportunity, the president of the Art Institute of Pittsburgh wrote him a letter and offered him a job as an instructor at the unbelievable salary of three hundred dollars per month! It was precisely what he had dreamed about since childhood. But somehow that letter became lost on the president's desk. The man later found and mailed it with another note saying he had wondered why my dad hadn't even paid him the courtesy of responding to his offer. But by the time the note came, my father had grown sick of himself and his lofty plans. He had found a place of prayer and yielded himself completely to the call of God on his life. So by the time the job offer came, he wrote back to say, 'Thanks, but I'm no longer interested.'

WHEN EVERYTHING TURNS ON ONE DECISION

My dad's future, and undoubtedly mine, hung in the balance at that critical juncture. If he had received the original offer from the president of AIP, he would have been launched on a career that was obviously out of the will of God. Who knows how his life would have changed if he had 'laboured in vain' in the wrong vineyard? What prevented him from making the mistake of his life? Well, my grandmother was out there praying for him every day, asking the Lord to draw her youngest son back to Himself. I believe God answered her prayers by interfering with the delivery of the letter on which everything seemed to depend.

> *My Dad's future, and undoubtedly mine, hung in the balance at that critical juncture.*

Does it seem cruel of the Lord to deprive this young man of the one thing he most wanted? Good question! Why would God give him remarkable ability and then prevent him from using it? Well, as is always the case in His dealings with us, the Lord had my father's best interests at heart. And He took nothing away from him.

As soon as my dad yielded to the will of the Lord, his art was given back to him. He then used his talent in ministerial work all his life, and when he died he was chairman of the art department at a Christian college. He left beautiful paintings and sculptures throughout the United States. More importantly, thousands of people came to know Jesus Christ through the preaching ministry of my father. They will be in heaven because of the calling that was on his life.

> *Jesus Christ will ask you to put Him in first place, too.*

So the terrible struggle that occurred in my father's teens was not a cruel manipulation. It was a vitally important test of his commitment—a challenge to put God in first place. And because he passed that test, I am here writing to you today!

Jesus Christ will ask you to put Him in first place, too. He will be Lord of all, or not Lord at all. That does not mean you will be required to become a minister. Your calling will be unique. But I am certain that anything carried out selfishly and independent of His purposes will not satisfy you and will ultimately be done 'in vain.'

We'll talk about how to interpret the will of God and recognise His purposes in a later discussion. For now, we must set about the task of thinking through the challenges you are facing. A contractor would never begin a skyscraper without detailed architectural and engineering plans to guide his work. Likewise, people in the critical decade between age sixteen and twenty-six owe it to their future to figure out who they are and what they want out of life. Helping you do that is what this book is all about.

We'll proceed with a look at the major 'mudholes' that trap and hold the unwary traveller.

2

THE COURTROOM
OF THE MIND

We're going to deal now with the fine art of feeling 'dumb'. Most of us have become very skilled at doing this. In fact, it does appear at times like life is intentionally designed to strip us of dignity and make us look ridiculous.

My friend Mike would certainly agree. When he was a university student, he had one of those unexpected little experiences that make a person feel stupid. He was on campus at lunchtime one day and decided to eat at an outdoor fast-food restaurant. Mike ordered a hamburger, some French fries, and a chocolate milkshake. He walked away carrying his food, in addition to his briefcase, some computer reports, and a couple of books. Unfortunately, every table was in use, and he had no place to set down all his things.

Mike stood there watching the students who were eating and talking at their tables. While he waited for someone to leave, the smell of his food got the better of him. He bent down to take a sip of the milkshake he was carrying. But instead of getting the straw into his mouth, he jammed it up his nose. The natural reaction would be to pull the milkshake down and move the head up. That is exactly what Mike did, which proved to be a mistake. The straw remained stuck up his nose and came out of the milkshake.

And he had no hand available to remove it. There he stood in front of hundreds of his peers with a straw sticking out of his nose and chocolate milkshake dripping on his trousers.

It was just a brief moment in time and an event that no one will remember except Mike. But he will never forget it. Why? Because it made him feel like a complete idiot. Have you ever been through anything like that? I'll bet every reader could tell a similar story.

I remember a high school girl I'll call Mary Jane. She had secretly given her figure a little help by padding her bra with this and that. Then she made the mistake of going to the senior swim party—where the truth about Mary Jane bubbled to the surface. Everyone else thought it was funny. Mary Jane didn't laugh.

> *We are extremely sensitive in our relationships . . . We are easily embarrassed. We ar easily hurt.*

As painful as such circumstances can be, they are almost universal in human experience. We've all been there at one time or another. Mark Twain observed that human beings are the only animals who are known to blush—or need to. That's the way we are made. If I had to choose a single word to characterise our emotional apparatus, it would be *vulnerable*. We are extremely sensitive in our relationships with one another or to anything that would humiliate us. We are easily embarrassed. We are easily hurt. We are easily angered. We are easily wounded. And we often fall flat on our faces at the most inopportune moment.

This tendency to get ourselves into weird situations is illustrated by one of my favourite cartoons, as follows:[1]

Life has a way of hanging us in the trees every now and then, but that is according to plan. God intentionally made us vulnerable and sensitive. He could have designed us with entirely different characteristics just as easily. He could have

"His name's Bradshaw. He says he understands I came from a single parent den with inadequate role models. He senses that my dysfunctional behavior is shame based and codependent and he urges me to let my inner cub heal............ I say we eat him."

given us the strength of water buffaloes, the independence of tigers, and the aggressiveness of lions. That is, in fact, the way we like to think of ourselves. But Scripture tells a very different story. The Lord sees us—Are you ready for this?—

as sheep. That's not very flattering, but it's what we read in dozens of biblical references. For example:

PSALM 100:3   Know that the Lord is God. It is he who made us, and we are . . . the *sheep* of his pasture.

ISAIAH 53:6   We all, like *sheep,* have gone astray, each of us has turned to his own way.

JEREMIAH 50:6   My people have been lost *sheep*; their shepherds have led them astray and caused them to roam on the mountains.

EZEKIEL 34:11   This is what the Sovereign Lord says: I myself will search for my *sheep* and look after them.

MATTHEW 9:36   When [Jesus] saw the crowds, he had compassion on them, because they were harassed and helpless, like *sheep* without a shepherd.

JOHN 10:27   My *sheep* listen to my voice; I know them, and they follow me.

1 PETER 2:25   For you were like *sheep* going astray, but now you have returned to the Shepherd and Overseer of your souls.

SHEEP OF THE LORD'S PASTURE

What are the characteristics of sheep that remind the Lord of you and me? What is He really saying when He refers to us in that way? Well, shepherds and farmers tell us that these animals are virtually defenceless against predators, not very resourceful, inclined to follow one another into danger, and they are absolutely dependent on their human masters for safety. They are also inclined to follow one another into dangerous situations. Thus, when David wrote, 'We all, like sheep, have gone astray,' he was referring to our tendency to move as an unthinking herd and away from the watchful care of the Shepherd.

> *The pressure to conform . . . is even stronger than the need for security and well-being*

I observed this herd instinct a few years ago in a documentary on television. It was filmed in an abattoir where sheep were being slaughtered for the meat market. Huddled in pens outside were hundreds of these nervous animals. They seemed to sense danger in their unfamiliar surroundings. Then a gate was opened that led up a ramp and through a door to the right. In order to get the sheep to walk up that ramp, the handlers used what is known as a 'Judas goat'. This is a goat that has been trained to lead the sheep into the slaughterhouse. The goat did his job very efficiently. He confidently walked to the bottom of the ramp and looked back. Then he took a few more steps and stopped again. The sheep looked at each other skittishly and then began moving towards the ramp. Eventually, they followed the confident goat to the top, where he went through a little gate to the left, but they were forced to turn to the right and went to their deaths. It was a dramatic illustration of unthinking, herd behaviour and the deadly consequences it often brings.

THAT IRRESISTIBLE URGE TO FOLLOW

There is a striking similarity between the sheep who follow the Judas goat and teenagers who succumb to deadly peer pressure. They inject themselves with heroin, sniff 'crack', engage in dangerous sexual practices, drive while drinking and shoot at each other with automatic weapons. But why do they do such destructive things? Don't they care about their own lives and the future they are putting at risk? Most of them do. But the pressure to conform—to follow their leaders—is even stronger than the need for security and well-being. Adults have the same problem. As King David observed, we *all* like sheep have gone astray.

Why is the urge to follow so irresistible in the human personality? Because it is driven by extremely powerful needs for love, belonging, and acceptance. Those who are unable to satisfy these deep longings sometimes do not thrive physically. For example, it has been known for many years that babies who are not loved and touched can die very quickly of a strange illness called marasmus. Something similar occurs among deprived adults. During the Korean War in the early fifties, the Chinese Communists made use of a new technique called 'brainwashing' in their prison camps. It consisted of isolating the POWs from each other by removing their leaders and cutting the soldiers off from all meaning.

This is the way we are made—vulnerable, needy, and very dependent on one another.

They permitted discouraging mail to be delivered but withheld any good news or expressions of support from home. The prisoners were rewarded for 'ratting' on one another so that no one knew who he could trust. Their home country was mocked and criticised day and night. In short, the Communists sought to remove everything with which the men could identify and draw support. They were effectively isolated from each other and the world. The result? More than 3,000 battle-hardened soldiers lay down on their beds, pulled the blankets over their heads, and died. There was no known cause for their deaths except that they lost the will to live.

This is the way we are made—vulnerable, needy, and very dependent on one another. Some are more sensitive than others, of course, especially in the earliest years of childhood. Research shows that a surprisingly large percentage of fourth-grade girls, barely ten years old, consider themselves to be 'fat' and are trying to diet.[2] Isn't that incredible?

> *Elaine fought back the tears as she watched her daugher standing sadly at the fence.*

Kids who ought to be skipping and playing games and swinging on the swings are worrying about their bodies and how they appear to others. It shouldn't be surprising that some of them will develop eating disorders in later years, including anorexia and bulimia.

Even during the preschool period, you can see this powerful force working to influence behaviour. A member of our staff at Focus on the Family shared a story about his three-year-old daughter that illustrates the early need for love and belonging. Beverly lived in a neighbourhood that had older children who did not want her tagging along behind them. They could run faster, climb higher, and do everything better than she, and that fact had not escaped her notice.

One day, Bev came running into the house and shouted to her mother, 'Lollipop, Mummy! I want lollipop.'

Elaine went to the kitchen and handed Bev a lollipop. But the child said urgently, 'No, Mummy. I want lots of lollipops.'

By this time the mother knew that something was up, so she decided to play along with her daughter. She handed her five or six lollipops, and then watched at the window to see what she would do with them.

Beverly ran to a fence that bordered a field next to their house. Her friends were on the other side playing baseball. She stuck her arm through the fence and waved the lollipops at the children. But they didn't see her. They just went on with their game as though the little girl wasn't there. Then one of the kids looked over at her and saw that she was offering them something good. They all came running over and rudely snatched the lollipops out of her hand. Then without even thanking her, they went back to playing ball. Alas, little Beverly stood there alone, her gifts and her friends both gone.

Elaine fought back the tears as she watched her daughter standing sadly at the fence. The child had tried to buy acceptance, but it only brought her further rejection. How badly Beverly wanted the other kids to like her and include her in their games. What she learned that day, however, is that love can't be bought and bribery usually brings only disrespect. Millions of teenage girls have discovered that same principle when their boyfriends have said, 'If you really loved me, you would have sex with me.' Not wanting to be rejected, they gave away their most precious and intimate gift—only to have the guys leave them standing alone and dejected at the fence.

Children often do great damage to one another by their cruelty and ridicule. Consider this note given to me by the mother of a fourth-grade girl, for example. It was written by one of her classmates for no apparent reason:

> Awful Janet
> You the stinkest girl in this world. I hope you die but of course I suppose that's impossible. I've some ideals.
>
> 1. Play in the road
> 2. Cut your throad
> 3. Drink poison
> 4. Knife yourself
>
> Please do some of this you big fat Girl. We all hate you.

I'am praying Oh please lord let Janet die. Were in need of
fresh air. Did you hear me lord cause if you didn' will all die
with her here. See Janet, we're not all bad.

from Wanda Jackson

What is 'Awful Janet' to think about a note like this? She
may have the confidence to take it in stride. But if Wanda is
popular and Janet is not, the stage is set for considerable
pain. Notice that Wanda hit all the sensitive nerves. She
insulted Janet's physical appearance and implied that all the
other students think she stinks. Those two messages—
'you're ugly' and 'everyone hates you'—could scar a particularly sensitive child. They may remember it for a lifetime.

NO ONE IS IMMUNE TO
THE PAIN OF REJECTION

Ask any adult to relate a similar incident from childhood
and you'll get an immediate response. Most remember experiences that may have occurred decades ago. Comedians
make good use of these sensitive nerves to make us laugh
because as William Makepeace Thackeray observed,
'Humour is the mistress of tears'. Rodney Dangerfield
agreed and built his comedy routine around the line, 'I don't
get no respect'. He said he was so rejected as a child even his
yo-yo wouldn't come back. Joan Rivers said she was such a
'dog' as a young girl that her father had to throw a bone
down the aisle to get her married. The comedian who made
the most effective use of inferiority was the scrawny introvert, Woody Allen. The following story from his childhood
came alive when he used to tell it.

Woody was on his way to his violin lesson when he
passed the pool hall where 'Floyd' and his friends hung out.
They were stealing hubcaps (from moving cars). Floyd called

Woody an insulting name as he passed, and being a 'cocky kid', Woody announced that he didn't take that from anybody! He put down his violin case and said, 'If you want to address me, you will call me Master Haywood Allen.' Woody said he spent that winter in a wheelchair. A team of surgeons laboured to remove a violin from his skull. His only good fortune was that it wasn't a cello.

That strikes most people funny because we were all terrorised by 'Floyd' sometime during childhood. We also remember each failure and humiliation from the early years. When I was in the third grade, I was playing right field in a hotly contested baseball game. How clearly I recall that black day. A kid came up to bat and hit a ball straight at me. It was a simple little pop fly—and all I had to do was catch it. But there in front of five million fans, most of them girls, I let the ball drop right through my outstretched fingers. In fact, it jammed my thumb on its way to the ground. I can still hear the pounding feet of four base runners heading for home plate. In frustration, I grabbed the ball and threw it to the umpire, who stepped aside and let it roll at least a city block. 'Boooo!' yelled half the five million hostile fans. 'Yeaaa!' shouted the other half.

I bled and died out there in right field that afternoon. It was a lonely funeral. I was the only mourner. But after careful thought in the days that followed, I gave up baseball and have seldom returned to it. I've run track, played basketball, and enjoyed four years of college tennis, but baseball bit the dust for me out there in right field. If you go to that playground today and scratch around in the northeast corner, you'll find the bones of a brilliant baseball career that died before it ever got started.

Well, let's bring this discussion a little closer to home. When hundreds of early painful experiences like this are followed by a stormy adolescence, a 'crisis of confidence' can occur as one moves into the critical decade. That has a way of interfering with everything we try to do.

A CRISIS OF CONFIDENCE

Consider, for example, the role played by confidence in professional tennis matches. The best players don't always win. But the most confident usually do. Furthermore, it is not unusual for the advantage to swing back and forth between evenly matched opponents. One may win the first set 6-0 and then lose the second just as badly.

How do we account for this kind of turnaround? Everything occurring during the two sets remains the same. The players, their ability and experience, the court, the weather, the balls, the rackets, the wind, the crowd, and the net have not changed.

What, then, is the variable that takes a seasoned professional from dramatic success in the first set to total defeat in the second? It is the ebb and flow of confidence. It comes and goes during the course of an athletic contest. Sports commentators give this surge a name. They call it *momentum*—but it is really just the by-product of believing in oneself.

Do you believe in your ability to deal with the major challenges of life? If you don't, others won't either. They will watch you carefully to see what you think of yourself. After all, you're the best source of information on that subject. Your own insecurities and doubt will translate directly into the attitudes of your peers.

The best players don't always win.

Please understand that the characteristic I'm promoting is not one of haughtiness and pride. Conceit is a weird disease. It makes everyone sick except the guy who has it. Pride also gets us into a lot of trouble. As the mother whale said to her baby, 'When you get to the surface and start to blow, that's when you get harpooned!'

Not only do we tend to dislike those among us who are arrogant, but we know from Scripture that God also despises that characteristic. Many of the stories in the Bible describe prideful men and God's eventual judgement on them.

We read in the book of Proverbs that there are seven things God hates, and pride is listed first among them (see Proverbs 6:16–17 KJV). So please understand that I'm not suggesting that you develop an attitude of self-importance, independence, and arrogance. I'm not even talking about self-esteem, as it is often interpreted. We're focusing here on the inner peace that comes from knowing you're a child of God and can, with His help, handle whatever He asks of you. It is a refusal to wallow in the sewer of self-hatred. It is believing in your worth as a human being regardless of the pain and rejection inflicted on you by others. It is, in a word, confidence.

Let me conclude this discussion by offering two concepts that should be helpful.

1. What we have been talking about, indirectly, is a little voice deep within the human spirit that tells each of us, 'You are a fool. No one likes you, and for good reason. You're a loser. You'll fail at everything you try to do. Everyone else is made of the right stuff, but you're different. No one could really love you. Not even God cares.'

I'm here to tell you that the owner of that 'little voice' has been called 'the father of lies' (John 8:44). His purpose is to deceive, to destroy and to demoralise. And his best weapon against us is to create an internal war that rips us apart from within. Abraham Lincoln said, 'A house divided against itself cannot stand.' That is especially true when it occurs in the recesses of the mind.

Unfortunately, many of us cooperate with Satan in his efforts to depress us. Former first lady Eleanor Roosevelt once said that no one can make a fool of you without your permission. She was right. We are often our own worst enemies when it comes to the undermining of confidence.

Let me quote from my book, *Hide or Seek*, in which I described how this traitorous act of self-hatred can occur. I call it 'the Courtroom of the Mind'.

Let's suppose you are an adolescent girl. You are sixteen years old and your name is Helen Highschool. To be very honest, you are not exactly gorgeous. Your shoulders are rounded and you have trouble remembering to close your mouth when you're thinking. (That seems to worry your folks a lot.) There are pimples distributed at random over your forehead and chin, and your oversized ears keep peeking out from under the hair that should hide them. You think often about these flaws and have wondered, with proper reverence, why God wasn't paying attention when you were being assembled.

You have never had a real date in your life, except for that disaster last February. Your mum's friend, Mrs Nosgood, arranged a blind date that almost signalled the end of the world. You knew it was risky to accept, but you were too excited to think rationally. Charming Charlie arrived in high spirits expecting to meet the girl of his dreams. You were not what he had in mind. Do you remember the disappointment on his face when you shuffled into the living room? Remember how he told Mary Lou the next day that your braces stuck out further than your chest? Remember him saying you had so much bridgework in your mouth that he'd have to pay a toll to kiss you? Horrible! But the night of your date he didn't say anything. He just sulked through the evening and brought you home two hours early. And of course Mary Lou couldn't wait to tell you the following afternoon how much Charlie hated you. You lashed back in anger. You caught him in the hall and told him he wasn't too bright for a boy with a head shaped like a light bulb. But the hurt went deep. You despised all males for at least six months and thought your hormones would never make a comeback.

When you arrived home from school that afternoon, you went straight to your room without speaking to the family. You closed the door and sat on the bed. You thought about the injustice of it all, letting your young mind play hopscotch over the many painful little memories that refused to fade. In fact, it seemed as though you were suddenly on trial to determine your acceptability to the human race.

The attorney for the prosecution stood before the jury and began presenting incriminating evidence as to your unworthiness. He recalled that fourth-grade Valentine's Day party when your beautiful cousin, Ann, got thirty-four cards and two boxes of chocolates, most of them from love-sick boys. You got three cards—two from girls and one from your Uncle Albert in San Antonio. The jury shook their heads in sorrow. The attorney then described the day that a sixth-grade boy shared his ice-cream cone with Betty Brigden but said he'd 'catch the uglies' if you took a bite. You acted like you didn't hear him, but you went to the girl's toilet and cried until breaktime was over.

'Ladies and gentlemen of the jury,' said the attorney, 'these are the unbiased opinions of Helen's own generation. The entire student body of Washington High School obviously agrees. They have no reason to lie. Their views represent truth itself. This homely girl simply does not deserve to be one of us! I urge you to find her guilty this day!'

Then the attorney for the defence arose. He was a frail little man who stuttered when he spoke. He presented a few witnesses on your behalf, including your mum and dad—and Uncle Albert, of course.

'Objection, your honour!' shouted the prosecutor. 'These are members of her own family. They don't count. They're biased witnesses, and their opinions are untrustworthy.'

'Objection sustained,' quoted the judge. Your attorney,

flustered and disconcerted, then mentioned how you kept your room clean, and he made a big deal about that 'A' you got in a geography test last month. You saw the foreman of the jury suppress a yawn and the others showed signs of complete boredom.

'A-a-a-and so, l-l-ladies and gentlemen of the j-j-jury, I ask y-y-you to find this y-y-young lady in-innocent of the charges.'

The jury was gone for thirty-seven seconds before bringing in a verdict. You stood before them and recognised them all. There was last year's homecoming queen. There was the quarterback of the football team. There was the outstanding graduate of the senior class. There was the surgeon's handsome son. They all looked down at you with stern eyes, and suddenly shouted in one voice: **'Guilty as Charged, Your Honour!'** The judge then read your sentence:

'Helen Highschool, a jury of your peers has found you to be unacceptable to the human race. You are hereby sentenced to a life of loneliness. You will probably fail in everything you do, and you'll go to your grave without a friend in the world. Marriage is out of the question, and there will never be a child in your home. You are a failure, Helen. You're a disappointment to your parents and must be considered excess baggage from this point forward. This case is hereby closed.'

The dream faded, but the decision of the jury remained real. Your parents wondered why you were so irritable and mean during the weeks that followed. They never knew—and you didn't tell them—that you had been expelled from the world of the 'Beautiful People'.

I wish I could talk to all the Helens and Bobs and Suzies and Jacks who have also been found unacceptable in the courtroom of the mind. They may never know that the trial was rigged—that every member of the jury has been charged with the same offence—that the judge himself was convicted more than thirty years ago. I wish I could tell each teenager that we have all stood before the bar of injustice, and few have been acquitted. Some of the adolescent convicts will be 'pardoned' later in life, but a greater number will never escape the sentence of the judge! And the irony of it all is that we each conduct our own rigged trial. We serve as our own prosecutor, and the final sentence is imposed under our own inflexible supervision—with a little help from our 'friends', of course.

After all, the trial was rigged!

If you have put yourself on trial in the past, it's time for an executive pardon to clear you of all charges. The case against you was pure baloney!

2. Together, you and God are a majority. I'm reminded of an NBA rookie who played on the Chicago Bulls team in the prime of superstar Michael Jordan. During one particular game Jordan was unbelievable and scored a magnificent sixty-eight points. The rookie rode the bench until the last minute of the game, when the coach graciously sent him on. He made a single free throw during the final seconds of the contest. When interviewed in the post-game show, the rookie was very pleased with himself. 'Together,' he said, 'Michael Jordan and I scored sixty-nine points.'

And so it is in our relationship with the Lord. We're just rookies playing with the Legend. As long as He blesses our meagre talent, it will be sufficient. Someone composed a song years ago that captured this thought. It was titled, *Little is Much if God is in it.* The writer was saying that our inadequacies are irrelevant if the Lord chooses to add His blessing. The emphasis has always been on His strength, not on our accomplishments.

We are often our own worst enemies when it comes to the undermining of confidence.

Look, for example, at the men Jesus chose to be His twelve disciples. He knew they would someday have to carry the gospel to a hostile world. Indeed, the future of the church would rest on their shoulders.

AN UNBEATABLE COMBINATION

From a human perspective, Jesus should have selected the most powerful and gifted leaders of that day. But He was not interested in theologians, military heroes, and political potentates. Instead, Jesus assembled a ragtag band of unsophisticated people including several uneducated fishermen and a hated tax collector. But He used them to turn the world upside down.

We are now His chosen disciples—His common people. That's the way we should think of the challenges before us. When our little bit is combined with His greatness, the team is unbeatable.

One thing is certain from Scripture. The Lord does not want us to use our inadequacies as an excuse to bail out of responsibility. He made that abundantly clear in an early encounter with Moses, as described in the fourth chapter of Exodus. God had spoken to Moses from the burning bush and ordered him to tell Pharaoh that he must release the children of Israel. Moses lacked the confidence for the task, however, and he tried to wriggle out of it. He said, 'O Lord, I have never been eloquent, neither in the past nor since you have spoken to your servant. I am slow of speech and tongue.'

To that, the Lord replied, 'Now go; I will help you speak and will teach you what to say.'

But Moses squirmed again. 'O Lord,' he said, 'please send someone else to do it.'

What cowardice Moses was displaying! The God of the universe who created all heaven and earth had promised to go with him. Nevertheless, his own self-doubt caused his knees to buckle.

Did the Lord accept his excuse? Hardly! Exodus 4:14 tells us that 'the Lord's anger burned against Moses.'

> *Together, you and God are a majority.*

Have you ever said, 'I know what You want me to do, Lord, but I'm sorry. I'm just not good at that'? Lotsa luck to you. Our heavenly Father will not accept our excuses of inadequacy, either. He makes us the same offer of support He made to Moses and then expects us to pack our bags and go!

The apostle Paul modelled the correct attitude for us when he wrote, 'I can do everything through him who gives me strength' (Philippians 4:13). That's the formula for successful living. Forget the Courtroom of the Mind! You stand acquitted!

3

FOR LOVE
OF MONEY

I recently sat in the international airport in Atlanta, Georgia, eating a fat-free yoghurt and watching the busy people rushing to and fro. Fascinating little dramas were played out before me. A mother scurried past on her way to gate 92. Trailing far behind her was a toddler who couldn't care less about catching their plane. He was singing little songs and dawdling happily through the terminal. Mum finally turned around and tried to speed him up. No chance! As they disappeared into the crowd, he was ten feet behind his mama and still losing ground.

Then came a maintenance man en route to perhaps a broken pipe or a blown circuit. He wore a yellow rubber apron on which he had written the name 'Whippie'. I wondered how he got that nickname and why he wanted the world to know about it. If you're out there, Whippie—I noticed!

A teenage girl and her mother then walked by. They looked like they had been in a fight earlier that morning. Maybe it was the girl's weird hairdo that had set them on edge. Whatever started the battle, the kid apparently won it. Mum looked pretty haggard for so early in the day. The adolescent had obviously spent hours that morning trying to make herself look sexy and older than her years. She had succeeded. Hang in there, Mum!

Hundreds of other people hurried past my observation post before I finished the yoghurt. All of them were deep in thought—intent on getting somewhere quick and doing whatever they came to do. I couldn't help wondering who these human beings were and what concerns they carried on this day. Back in the 1960s, the Beatles rock group sang about, 'All the lonely people, where do they all come from.'[1] Yes, I saw a few folks who looked like they desperately needed a friend. But mostly, I saw busy, exhausted men and women who appeared to be hours behind schedule. Would it really have created an international crisis if they had pulled up a chair beside me and watched the people go by for a few minutes? I know! I know! Planes don't wait.

Life in the fast lane is coming your way. I guarantee it.

What I witnessed in Atlanta airport is characteristic of the modern way of doing things. You may not yet be caught up in it, having so recently enjoyed the carefree days of adolescence. But life in the fast lane is coming your way—I guarantee it. The frantic pace of living that almost deprives us of meaning is very contagious, and most people find themselves on its treadmill sooner or later.

LIFE'S REALLY BIG QUESTIONS

It is so important to pause and think through some basic issues while you are young, before the pressures of job and family become distracting. There are several eternal questions everyone must deal with eventually. You will benefit, I think, from doing that work now.

Whether you are an atheist, a Muslim, a Buddhist, a Jew, a New-Ager, an agnostic, or a Christian, the questions confronting the human family are the same. Only the answers will differ. They are:

Who am I as a person?
How did I get here?
What really matters to me?
Is Someone keeping score?
What does He expect of me?
Is there life after death?
How do I achieve eternal life, if it exists?
What is the meaning of death?

We will deal presently with many of the important questions. For now, let's focus on another that is foundational: What goals are worthy of the investment of my life? These should be resolved before pressing any further into adulthood.

GAME-SHOW GREED

When it comes to purposes and goals, most people appear motivated primarily by the pursuit of money and the things it can buy. If you doubt that, turn on daytime television and watch the contestants as they compete for prizes and cash. Observe the 'cuckoo birds' as they leap in the air, frothing at the mouth and tearing at the clothes of the host. Notice that their eyes are dilated and their ears are bright pink. It's a condition known as *game-show greed*, and it renders its victims incapable of rational judgement.

> *Yes, **Betty Molino, you** have won a **new washing machine,** a year's supply of **chewy chocolate bars,** and this marvellous new doll, **Wanda wee-wee,** that actually soaks your daughter's lap! **Congragulations, Betty,** and thanks for playing 'Grab Bag' (frantic applause).*

How do I know so much about game-show greed? Because I've been there! Back in 1967, my lovely wife managed to drag me to the 'Let's Make a Deal' show, which was the rage at that time. Shirley put toy birds all over her head and blouse, and I carried a sign that said, 'My wife is for the birds'. Really funny, huh? It was good enough to get the host, Monty Hall, to choose us as lucky contestants. The producers placed us in the two front seats near the cameras but began the programme by 'dealing' with other suckers.

I kept thinking as I sat there in the contestants' row, *What in the world am I doing here holding this stupid sign?* I couldn't have been more sceptical about the proposition. Finally, Monty called our names, and the cameras zoomed in.

'Here behind door number one is . . . *(a curtain opens) . . . A Neeeew Caar!!*' *(The audience goes crazy with excitement.)*

Suddenly, I was gripped by a spasm in the pit of my stomach. My mouth watered profusely, and my heart began knocking on the sides of my chest. There on that stage was the car of my dreams—a brand-new Camaro. Desire came charging up my throat and stuck in the region of my Adam's apple. My breathing became irregular and shallow, which was another unmistakable clue that I had been struck by game-show greed.

To understand this reaction, you would have to know that I have owned several of the worst cars in automotive history. Throughout my college years I drove a 1949 Mercury convertible (I called it Ol' Red) that had power seats, power windows, power top, power everything—but no power to run them. I put the windows up in the winter and down in the summer. There they remained, despite fluctuating temperatures. Shirley, who was then my girl-friend, must have loved me tremendously to have put up with that car. She *hated* it! The front seat had a spring with a bad temper that tore her clothes and punctured her skin. Nor did Ol' Red always choose to run. Every few days, Shirley and I would take this junk heap out for a push.

WHY I WANTED THAT NEW CAR

The final blow occurred shortly after our graduation from college. We were invited to appear for important job interviews, and we put on our Sunday best for the occasion. There we were, suit and tie, heels and hose, going sixty miles an hour down the road in Ol' Red, when the convertible top suddenly blew off. Strings and dust flapped in our face as the canvas waved behind the car like Superman's cape. The ribs of the top protruded above our heads, reminiscent of under-sized roll-bars. It was very embarrassing. And can you believe that Shirley got mad at *me* for letting that happen? She crouched on the floor, blaming me for driving such a beat-up car. It is a miracle that our relationship survived that emotional afternoon.

There on that stage was the car of my dreams— a brand new Camaro.

Although Ol' Red had been put to sleep long before our appearance on 'Let's Make a Deal', I still had never owned a new car. Every available dollar had been allocated for tuition in graduate school. I had finished my Ph.D just two months earlier.

This explains my reaction to the beautiful automobile behind door number one.

'All you have to do to win the car,' said Monty, 'is tell us the prices of four items.'

Shirley and I guessed the first three but blew it on number four. 'Sorry,' said Monty. 'You've been "zonked". But here, take a vacuum cleaner and three dollars. And thanks for playing 'Let's Make a Deal'!

Shirley and I were just sick. On the way home we talked

about how our emotions had been manipulated in that situation. We both experienced incredible greed, and the feeling was uncomfortable. I have since learned a very valuable lesson about lust and how it operates in a spiritual context. It has been my observation that whatever a

> *Whatever a person hungers for, Satan will appear to offer.*

person hungers for, Satan will appear to offer in exchange for a spiritual compromise. In my case, a new automobile was the perfect enticement to unleash my greed. If illicit sex is your desire, it will eventually be made available. Don't be surprised when you are beckoned by a willing partner.

If your passion is for fame or power, that object of lust will be promised (even if never delivered).

Remember that Jesus was offered bread following His forty-day fast in the wilderness. He was promised power and glory after He had been contemplating His forthcoming road to the cross. My point is that Satan uses our keenest appetites to tempt us.

WATCH OUT! TEMPTATION AHEAD!

Likewise, if you hunger and thirst for great wealth—beware! You are in a very precarious position. If you doubt it, look at 1 Timothy 6:9, which says, 'People who want to get rich fall into temptation and a trap and into many foolish and harmful desires that plunge men into ruin and destruction.' What incredible insight into the nature of mankind. If you watch people who care passionately about money, you'll observe that many of them are suckers for wild-eyed schemes and shady deals. They are always on the verge of a bonanza that seems to slip through their fingers. Instead of getting rich, they just get taken.

Billionaire John D. Rockefeller had some cogent advice

for those who wanted to be rich. 'It's easy,' he said. 'All you have to do is get up early, work hard—and strike oil.' Easy for him to say.

This discussion reminds me of a deer-hunting trip I took with my son when he was a teenager. We got into the stand very early in the morning before the sun came up. About twenty yards away from us was a feeder that operated on a timer. At 7.00 a.m. it automatically dropped kernels of corn into a dish below.

Ryan and I huddled together in the stand, talking softly about whatever came to mind. Then, through the fog, we saw a beautiful doe emerge silently into the clearing. She took nearly thirty minutes to get to the feeder near where we were hiding. We had no intention of shooting her, but it was fun to watch this beautiful animal from close range. She was extremely wary, sniffing the air and listening for the sounds of danger. Finally, she inched her way to the feeder, still looking around skittishly as though sensing our presence. Then she ate a quick breakfast and fled.

I whispered to Ryan, 'There is something valuable to be learned from what we have just seen. Whenever you come upon a free supply of high-quality corn, provided unexpectedly right there in the middle of the forest, be careful! The people who put it there are probably sitting nearby in a stand, just waiting to take a shot at you. Keep your eyes and ears open!'

The greedier you become, the more vulnerable you are to the conmen of our time.

Ryan may not always remember that advice, but I will. It isn't often that a father says something to his teenage son that he considers to be profound, and it applies to you. The greedier you become, the more vulnerable you are to the 'con' men of our time. They will bait the trap with high-quality 'corn', whether it be money, sex, an attractive job offer or flattery. You'll hardly be able to believe your eyes. What a deal! But take care! Your pretty head may already be in the scope of someone's rifle.

Not only are there pitfalls for those who seek riches, but the few who acquire them are in for a disappointment. They quickly learn that wealth will not satisfy their need for significance. No amount of money will do that.

A popular car bumper sticker reads, 'He who dies with the most toys, wins.' It's a lie. It should read, 'He who dies with the most toys, dies anyway.' I hope you will believe me when I say that a lifetime invested in the accumulation of things will have been wasted. There *has* to be a better reason for living than that.

MONEY:
JESUS' MOST TALKED-ABOUT TOPIC

Jesus' own teachings have great relevance for us at this point. Have you ever wondered what topic He talked about more often than any other? Was it heaven, hell, sin, repentance, love, or His second coming? No, it was money, and most of what He said came in the form of a warning. This caution about possessions and riches appeared throughout Jesus' teachings. Here are just a few passages from one of the four Gospels, the book of Luke:

Jesus said to a crowd of His followers, 'But woe to you who are rich, for you have already received your comfort' (Luke 6:24).

He also said, 'Watch out! Be on your guard against all kinds of greed; a man's life does not consist in the abundance of his possessions' (Luke 12:15).

Jesus told a parable about a rich fool who had no need of God. The man believed he had many years to live and said to himself, 'You have plenty of good things laid up for many years. Take life easy; eat, drink and be merry.' But God said to him, 'You fool! This very night your life will be demanded from you. Then who will get what you have prepared for yourself?' Jesus ended the parable with this sober warning, 'This is how it will be with anyone who stores up things for himself but is not rich towards God' (Luke 12:18–21).

Jesus later visited the home of a prominent Pharisee and said to His host, 'When you give a luncheon or dinner, do not invite your friends, your brothers or relatives, or your rich neighbours; if you do, they may invite you back and so you will be repaid. But when you give a banquet, invite the poor, the crippled, the lame, the blind, and you will be blessed' (Luke 14:12–14).

He told a parable of the prodigal son who demanded his inheritance early and then squandered it on prostitutes and riotous living (see Luke 15:11–31).

Jesus said to His disciples, 'No servant can serve two masters. Either he will hate the one and love the other, or he will be devoted to the one and despise the other. You cannot serve both God and Money' (Luke 16:13).

He told a parable of the rich man who had everything. The man was clothed in fine purple and linen, and he ate the very best food. But he was unconcerned about the misery of the beggar Lazarus, who was hungry and covered with sores. The rich man died and went to hell where he was tormented, but Lazarus was taken to heaven where he was comforted (see Luke 16:19).

He spoke to a rich young ruler and commanded him to sell all he had and give it to the poor. The man went away very sorrowfully 'because he was a man of great wealth' (Luke 18:18–23).

Finally, Jesus turned to His disciples and said, 'How hard it is for the rich to enter the kingdom of God! Indeed, it is easier for a camel to go through the eye of a needle than for a rich man to enter the kingdom of God' (Luke 18:24).

Isn't it incredible how many of Jesus' statements dealt with money in one way or another? We must ask ourselves why. Is there a reason the Master kept returning to that theme? Of course there is. Jesus was teaching us that great spiritual danger accompanies the pursuit and the achievement of wealth. He explained why in Matthew 6:21, 'For where your treasure is, there your heart will be also.'

GIVE THE LORD FIRST PLACE

Remember my statement in the first chapter that the Lord will not settle for second place in your life. That is the threat posed by money. It can become our treasure—our passion—our greatest love. And when that happens, God becomes almost irrelevant.

Now, what does this understanding mean in today's world? Are we prohibited from earning a living, owning a home and car, having a savings account? Certainly not. In fact, we read in 1 Timothy 5:8, 'If anyone does not provide for his relatives, and especially for his immediate family, he has denied the faith and is worse than an unbeliever.' Men, specifically, are required to provide for and protect their families, which requires them to bring in money from their labours.

> *Great spiritual danger accompanies the pursuit and the achievement of wealth.*

Wealth is not an evil in itself, either. Abraham, David, and other great men of the Bible were blessed with riches. And in fact, the Scriptures indicate that God gives to some people the power to acquire wealth (see Deuteronomy 8:18 and 1 Samuel 2:7). Then where is the point of danger? The apostle Paul clarified for us that money is not the problem. It is the *love* of money that is the root of all evil (see 1

Timothy 6:10). We get into trouble when our possessions become a god to us.

What, then, is the biblical approach to possessions and money? We've seen what is wrong, but what is right? According to Christian financial counsellor and author Ron Blue, there are four principles for money management that are foundational. If they are implemented in your life, you'll never have a problem with materialism. Let's look at them quickly:

> *The Lord will not settle for second place in your life.*

Principle 1. God owns it all.

Some people have the notion that the Lord is entitled to ten per cent of our income, known as 'tithes', and that the other ninety per cent belongs to us. Not true. I believe strongly in the concept of tithing, but not because God's portion is limited to a tenth. We are but stewards of all that He has entrusted to us. He is our possessor—and sometimes our dispossessor. Everything we have is but a loan from Him. When God took away his wealth, Job had the correct attitude, saying, ' "Naked I came from my mother's womb, and naked I will depart." The Lord gave and the LORD has taken away; may the name of the LORD be praised' (Job 1:21).

If you understand this basic concept, it becomes clear that every spending decision is a spiritual decision. Waste, for example, is not a squandering of our resources. It is a poor use of His.

> *Every spending decision is a spiritual decision.*

Expenditures for worthwhile purposes, such as holidays, ice-cream, bicycles, blue jeans, magazines, tennis rackets, cars, and hamburgers, are also purchased with His money. That's why in my family, we bow to thank the Lord before eating each meal. Everything, including our food, is a gift from His hand.

Principle 2. There is always a trade-off between time and effort and money and rewards.

You've heard the phrases, 'There's no such thing as a free lunch', and 'You can't get something for nothing'. Those are very important understandings. Money should always be thought of as linked to work and the sweat of our brow.

Here's how this second principle has meaning for us. Think for a moment of the most worthless, unnecessary purchase you have made in recent years. Perhaps it was an electric shaver that now sits in the garage, or an article of clothing that will never be worn. It is important to realise that this item was not purchased with your money; it was bought with your time, which you traded for money. In effect, you swapped a certain proportion of your allotted days on earth for that piece of junk that now clutters your home.

When you understand that everything you buy is purchased with a portion of your life, it should make you more careful with the use of money.

Principle 3. There is no such thing as an independent financial decision.

There will never be enough money for everything you'd like to buy or do. Even billionaires have some limitations on their purchasing power. Therefore, every expenditure has implications for other things you need or want. It's all linked together. What this means is that those who can't resist blowing their money on junk are limiting themselves in areas of greater need or interest.

And by the way, husbands and wives often fight over the use of money. Why? Because their value systems differ and they often disagree on what is wasteful. My mother and father were typical in this regard. If Dad spent five dollars for shotgun shells or for tennis balls, he justified the expenditure because it brought him pleasure. But if Mum bought a five-dollar potato peeler that wouldn't work, he considered that wasteful. Never mind the fact that she enjoyed shopping as much as he did hunting or playing tennis. Their perspectives were simply unique. This is a potential problem you and your future spouse will just have to work through.

Again, this third principle involves a recognition that an extravagance at one point will eventually lead to frustration at another point. Good business managers are able to keep the main picture in mind as they make their financial decisions.

Principle 4. Delayed gratification is the key to financial maturity.

Since we have limited resources and unlimited choices, the only way to get ahead financially is to deny ourselves some of the things we want. If we don't have the discipline to do that, then we will always be in debt. Remember too that unless you spend less than you earn, no amount of income will be enough. That's why some people receive salary increases and soon find themselves even deeper in debt.

Let me repeat this important concept: No amount of income will be sufficient if spending is not brought under control. Consider the finances of the United States government, for example. It extracts more than a trillion dollars annually from American taxpayers. That's a thousand billion bucks! But our Congress spends hundreds of billions more than that.

Even by the most liberal interpretation, much of this revenue is wasted on programmes that don't work and on unnecessary and expensive bureaucracies. Consequently, the size of our national debt is

Unless you spend less than you earn, no amount of income will be enough!

mind-boggling. The point is inescapable: Whether it be within a government or by a private individual, there must be a willingness to deny short-term gratification and to live within one's means. It isn't easy, but it pays big dividends at maturity.[2]

A SOLID FINANCIAL FOUNDATION

Well, maybe these four principles will help you build a foundation of financial stability without compromising your belief system. In short, the secret of successful living is to spend your life on something that will outlast it, or, as the writer to the Hebrews said, 'Keep your lives free from the love of money and be content with what you have' (Hebrews 13:5).

Let's return to the question with which we began: What goals are worthy of the investment of your life? We haven't answered it definitively, but we've eliminated money as a worthy objective. We'll look at another alternative in the next chapter.

4

THE
POWERBROKERS

We have been talking about the basic motivtors of human behaviour and how they relate to the choices that must be made during the critical decade. One of them, the pursuit of money, has been discredited (I hope) as a valid reason for living. Now we will look at another driving force that is even more influential in shaping the way things work. I'm referring to the pursuit of power. The lust for it permeates human societies and has its origins very early n life.

A child between eighteen and thirty-six months of age is a skilled powerbroker. They love to run things—and break things, squash things, flush things and eat horrible things. Comedian Bill Cosby once said, 'Give me 200 active two-year-olds, and I could conquer the world.' It's true. Toddlers, in their cute, charming way, can be terrors. They honestly believe the universe revolves around them, and they like it that way.

I remember a three-year-old who was sitting on his potty when a huge earthquake shook the city of Los Angeles. Dishes were crashing and furniture was skidding across the floor. The little boy hung on to his potty-chair and said to his mother, 'What did I do, Mum?' It was a logical question from his point of view. If something important had happened, he must have been responsible for it.

This heady confidence lasts but a few short years, as we have seen. It gives way to self-doubt and insecurity. Alas, one of the most uncomfortable features of adolescence is the sense of powerlessness it can bring. One mother told me that her seventh-grade daughter was being ridiculed at school every day. She said the girl woke an hour before she had to get up each morning and lay there thinking about how she could get through her day without being humiliated. Millions of teenagers could identify with her.

Other adolescents resent the fact that their parents hold all the power. As minors, they can't vote, drive, drink, have sex, or run their own lives—unless they break the rules. Some of them resent this situation and refuse to accept it. This leads to rebellion with which we are all familiar. It is an early grab for power instead of waiting to inherit it naturally in your twenties. Some tragic mistakes are often made by those who acquire the reins of control before their maturity is adequate to handle it.

POWER AND ADOLESCENT RELATIONSHIPS

It is impossible to understand adolescent society without comprehending the role of power in interpersonal relationships. You have recently been there and should be able to recall that competitive environment. That is the heart and soul of its value system. It comes in various forms, of course. For girls, there is no greater social dominance than physical beauty. A truly gorgeous young woman is so powerful that even the boys are often afraid of her. She rules in a high school setting like a queen on a throne, and in fact, she is usually granted a title with references to royalty in its name (Homecoming Queen, All-School Queen, Sweetheart Queen, Football Queen, Prom Queen, etc.). The way she uses that status with her peers is fascinating to those of us who are interested in human behaviour.

For boys, power games are much more physical than for girls. The bullies literally stuff their will down the throats of those who are weaker. That is what I remember from my own high school years. I had a number of fights during that era just to defend my 'turf'. There was one guy, however, whom I had no intention of tackling. His name was McKeechern, but we called him 'Killer'. He was the terror of the town. Everyone believed Killer would dismantle anyone who crossed him. That theory was never tested to my knowledge. At least, not until I blundered into a confrontation.

> *A truly gorgeous young woman is so powerful that even the boys are often afraid of her.*

When I was fifteen years old and an impulsive student, I nearly ended a long and happy manhood before it had a chance to get started. As I recall, a blizzard had blown through our State the night before and a group of us had gathered in front of the school to throw snowballs at passing cars. (Does that tell you anything about our collective maturity at the time?) Just before the afternoon bell rang, I looked up the street and saw McKeechern chugging along in his 'chopped' 1934 Chevy. It was a junk heap with a cardboard 'window' on the driver's side. McKeechern had cut a three-by-three-inch flap in the cardboard, which he lifted when turning left. You could see his evil eyes peering out just before he went around corners. When the flap was down, however, he was unaware of things happening on the left side of the car. As luck would have it, that's where I was standing with a huge snowball in my hand—thinking very funny and terribly unwise thoughts.

If I could just go back to that day and counsel myself, I would say, *Don't do it, Jim! You could lose your sweet life right*

here. McKeechern will tear your tongue out if you hit him
with that snowball. Just put it down and go quietly to your
afternoon class. Please, son! If you lose, I lose! Unfortunately,
no such advice wafted to my ears that day, and I didn't have
the sense to realise my danger. I heaved the snowball into
the upper atmosphere with all my might. It came down just
as McKeechern drove by and, unbelievably, went through
the flap in his cardboard window. The missile obviously hit
him squarely in the face, because his Chevy wobbled all
over the road. It bounced over the curb and came to a stop
just short of the school building.

Killer exploded from the front seat, ready to rip someone
(me!) to shreds. I'll never forget the sight. There was snow
all over his face and little jets of steam were curling from his
head. My whole life passed in front of my eyes as I faded
into the crowd. *So young!* I thought.

The only thing that saved me on this snowy day was
McKeechern's inability to identify me. No one told him I
had thrown the snowball, and believe me, I didn't volunteer.
I escaped unscathed, although that brush with destiny must
have made a great impact on me emotionally. I still have
recurring nightmares about the event all these years later. In
my dreams, the chimes ring and I go to open the front door.
There stands McKeechern with a shotgun. And he still has
snow on his face. (If you read this story, Killer, I do hope we
can be friends. We were only kids, you know? No offence,
right? Howsa car?)

THE LIFELONG QUEST FOR POWER

Why have I described the power struggles of the adolescent
years in this detail? What does this turbulent period have to
do with the critical decade and beyond? Well, it is highly
relevant to the issues at hand and figures prominently in

your own future. As I have indicated, the quest for power is a lifelong passion for many people. It takes different forms in the adult years, but the emotional wellspring is the same. Most of us want to run things. Even the desire for money discussed in the last chapter is a function of this longing for control and influence. Why? Because those with the most money are perceived as being the most powerful.

I still have recurring night-mares. . . all these years later.

Just how important is raw power in your own motivation? Will it shape your choice of career? Do you hope to be a doctor, lawyer, military officer, or politician because these professions represent influence in our culture? Are you determined to make a name for yourself? Do you want people to say when you pass, 'There goes a great person'? Do you hope they'll want your autograph and your photograph? Is your purpose in living to be found in these symbols of significance?

If so, your ladder is leaning against the wrong wall. But let me hasten to clarify. God has given you talent, and He wants you to use it productively. You should set your goals high and direct your energies towards achieving them. Train your mind. Develop your skills. Discipline your appetites. Prepare for the future. Work hard. Go for it! You can't steal second with one foot on first.

But before you set out to make your mark, you should ask yourself, 'For *whom* will this be done?' If you seek power so you can be powerful, you're on the wrong track. If you crave fame to become famous, the journey will be disappointing. If you desire influence so you can be influential, you're making a big mistake. This is what the Lord says about these trappings of success: 'Let not the wise man glory in his wisdom, neither let the mighty man glory in his might, let not the rich man glory in his riches' (Jeremiah 9:23 KJV). What then should we glory in? The apostle Paul provides the answer: 'So whether you eat or drink or whatever you do, do it all for the glory of God' (1 Corinthians 10:31).

That's very clear, isn't it? Our purposes are not our own. They are His. Thus, the choice of an occupation and 'whatever you do' is to be motivated by your service to the kingdom of God. That is the only thing that carries eternal significance. Nothing else will satisfy. Everything else is going to burn.

I have lived long enough to see some of my early dreams of glory come unstitched. One of them began shortly after I graduated from high school and went off to college. I arrived on campus several days before classes started and walked around looking at the place that would be my home for the next four years. I was like a tourist on holiday.

Of greatest interest to me that morning was the trophy cabinet standing in the main administration building. There behind the glass were the glitzy symbols of past athletic victories. Basketball, track, and baseball were well represented. Then I saw it. Standing majestically at the centre of the case was the perpetual tennis trophy. It was about two feet tall and had a shiny little man on top. Engraved on the shaft were the names of all the collegiate tennis champions back to 1947. Every one of those heroes was burned into my memory. I could name most of them today.

> 'Whatever you do' is to be motivated by your service to the kingdom of God.

As I stood there before that historic trophy, I said to myself, *Someday! Some fine day I'm going to add my name to that list of legends.* I set my jaw, determined to show the world.

As strange as it may seem today, becoming our college tennis champ was my highest goal in life at that time. Nothing could have mattered more to me. Tennis had been my passion in high school. I had played six days a week for eleven months of each year. When I graduated and headed for college, it was with the intention of riding this sport into the record books.

Well, I did have a certain amount of success with my tennis career. I lettered all four years, captained the team as a senior, and yes, I got my name inscribed on the big trophy. In fact, I did it twice during each of my last two seasons. I left the college with the satisfaction of knowing that future generations of freshmen would stand at the display case and read my name in admiration. Someday they may be great like me.

WHERE'S THAT TROPHY NOW?

Alas, about fifteen years later a friend had reason to visit the college I attended. He was dumping something in the rubbish bin behind the administration building, and what do you suppose he found? Yep, there among the refuse and debris was the perpetual tennis trophy! The athletic department had actually thrown it away! What a blow! There I was, a legend in my own time, and who cared? Some universities retire the jersey numbers of their greatest athletes. My school didn't retire my number. They retired my memory!

The friend, Dr Wil Spaite, who had been one of my team-mates in college, took the tennis trophy home and cleaned it up. He put a new shiny man on the top and bought a new base for it. Then he gave it to me to commemorate our 'prime', which everyone appeared to have forgotten. That trophy stands in my office today. I'll show it to you if you come by for a visit. My name is on it twice. You'll be impressed. It was a big deal at the time. Honest.

This brief encounter with fame has taught me a valuable

lesson about success and achievement. Pay attention now, because this could be on the mid-term: **If you live long enough, life will trash your trophies, too.** I don't care how important something seems at the time, if it is an end in itself, the passage of time will render it old and tarnished. Who cares today that Zachary Taylor or William Henry Harrison won their elections for president of the United States? Can you name three US senators in the year 1933? Probably not, and who cares anyway? What difference did it make that the Brooklyn Dodgers defeated the Yankees in the 1955 World Series? The hero of that series, Sandy Amoros, made a game-saving catch that a nation cheered, but he was soon penniless, forgotten, and living on the streets.[1]

John Gilbert was the biggest romantic male film star of the 1920s. He was by far the highest-paid actor in Hollywood, and his name was given top billing in every film in which he starred. Almost everyone in the country knew his name. But within two years, no studio would hire him. Gilbert died in 1936 from a heart attack brought on by alcohol and drug abuse. He was just thirty-six years old.[2] Have you ever heard of him? I doubt it. My point is that even the most awesome triumphs lose their sizzle in time.

Let me bring the matter closer to home. In November 1974, the University of Southern California's football team played their historic rival, Notre Dame, at the Coliseum in Los Angeles. It was one of the most exciting games in history, especially for USC fans. I attended graduate school at USC, and I still get very 'jazzed' about its football games. And there are very few pleasures more gratifying for me than beating the socks off Notre Dame! (Supporters of the Irish will just have to forgive me.)

Well, that November day in '74 produced one of the greatest football games of all times. Notre Dame ripped through the Trojans in the first half, leading 24–6 at half-time. I don't know what Coach John McKay said to his team in the locker room, but something set USC on fire. They were an entirely different team in the second half. A tailback named Anthony (A.D.) Davis took the opening kick-off eighty-five yards for a touchdown. That started one of the most unbelievable comebacks in the history of the series. By the final gun, 'A.D.' had scored four touchdowns, and USC had put 54 points on the board.

I was watching the game on television that afternoon. There I was in my study, cheering and screaming as though I was surrounded by 100,000 fans in the Coliseum. I never sat down through the second half! It was some kind of day.

A. D. Davis was the hero of the game, of course. He was on talk shows, and his picture was on virtually every sports page in the country the next morning. He had his day in the sun, to be sure. Football fans everywhere were talking about Anthony and his four explosive touchdowns.

Well, many years went by, and USC was again engaged in another make-or-break football game. This time the opponent was UCLA, and the winner would be going to the Rose Bowl on 1 January, 1990. I was on the sidelines that day as the Trojans pulled off another miracle and scored a last-minute touchdown to win. The athletic director at that time, Mike McGee, is a friend of mine, and he invited me into the locker room after the game. It was another wonderful victory in the history of USC football. The two heroes of the day, Rodney Peete and Eric Afhaulter, were hoisted onto the shoulders of their team-mates, and everyone was singing the 'Trojan fight song'. It was a fine experience just being there.

Then I was distracted momentarily and looked to my left. There in the shadows was A. D. Davis, the superstar of 1974. He was watching the hullabaloo from the sidelines. I don't mean to be disrespectful to him because it happens to all of us, but A. D. didn't look like the finely tuned athlete I remembered from the past. He had put on some weight and had acquired a little belly that wasn't there in his prime. Here was 'Mr Yesterday', watching the new whiz kids and probably remembering what it was like to be in the spotlight. But his time on centre stage had come and gone, and now—what did it really matter?

SUCCESS, TOO, WILL FADE

That's the way the system works. Your successes will fade from memory, too. That doesn't mean you shouldn't try to achieve them. But it should lead you to ask, 'Why are they important to me? Are my trophies for me, or are they for Him?' These are critical questions that every believer is obligated to answer.

Permit me one more illustration that relates not to sports but to the acquisition of political power. We've seen that the desire for influence and control is basic to the human personality, especially among men. But how much satisfaction does it bring to those who achieve it? I would not deny that authority is intoxicating for some people and that they crave the perks that go with it. Nevertheless, power is at best a temporary phenomenon that eventually must be surrendered. That brings me to this final illustration.

Gary Bauer, president of the Family Research Council in Washington, DC, served for eight years in the Reagan White House. He was chief domestic policy adviser during the latter part of that era and worked in a beautiful panelled office near the president. His boss was a man named Donald Regan, Chief of Staff for the administration. Regan was one tough customer! He was a no-nonsense executive who intimidated those who worked for him. It was a fearful thing to be called into his office for a reprimand. Regan was at the pinnacle of world power, representing the president and sharing his awesome authority.

One day, Gary was sick with flu and stayed home in bed. He was watching CNN on television and learned, unbelievably, that Don Regan had been summarily fired by President Reagan. As it was later learned, Mr Regan had made the mistake of irritating Nancy Reagan, and she saw to it that he was sacked. Recognising that everything was up for grabs, Gary got out of bed despite a 102-degree fever and drove to Washington. He parked his car and walked through the main gate of the White House. There he met Don Regan coming out the front entrance. Incredibly, he was carrying his own boxes. He had been one of the most powerful men in the world two hours earlier; now he didn't even have anyone to help him clean out his office. Regan had been watching the same CNN broadcast that Gary had seen. That's how he learned he had been fired. Suddenly, it was over. He was a has-been. So much for the permanence and reliability of power!

> *Your success will fade from memory.*

I'm sure you see the relevance of these examples to your life, but let me leave no doubt. If the triumphs of the world's superstars and powerbrokers so quickly turn to dust, how much less significant will be the modest achievements you and I will be likely to garner? If our successes are simply ends in themselves, are they worth the investment of our years? Do they justify our brief tenure on this mortal coil? Is that all there is to a fire? I believe most passionately that it is not!

There was an incident in Scripture that puts this discussion into perspective. It is reported in 1 Chronicles 28, when King David had grown old and knew he was dying. He called together his officials, military leaders, business managers, and 'mighty men' to hear his final words. In the assembly that day was his son Solomon, whom God had designated to succeed David as king. A very touching and historic conversation then occurred between the dying monarch and his young heir.

SOUND ADVICE FROM A
DYING KING

The advice David gave that day was of great significance, not only for Solomon but also for you and me. A person doesn't waste words when the angel of death hovers nearby. Picture the scene, then, as the old man offers his last thoughts to his beloved son who would carry on his legacy. This is what David said, probably with strong feeling and a shaky voice:

> And thou, Solomon my son, know thou the God of thy father, and serve him with a perfect heart and with a willing mind: for the Lord searcheth all hearts, and understandeth all the imaginations of the thoughts: if thou seek him, he will be found of thee; but if thou forsake him, he will cast thee off forever (1 Chronicles 28:9 KJV).

A lifetime of wisdom was packed into that brief statement from the godly king. Notice first that David advised Solomon to 'know' God. He didn't say 'know about God.' I know about Abraham Lincoln, but I never met him. David wanted Solomon to be acquainted personally with the God of Israel, whom he had tried to serve with a willing mind.

Then the king laid before his son the fundamental issue facing every person who ever lived. He said, 'If thou seek him, he will be found of thee; but if thou forsake him, he will cast thee off for ever.' If I had a thousand years to consider a final message for my son or daughter, I couldn't improve on these last words of David.

It is also my best advice to you as we conclude this discussion of purposes and goals. Whatever else you set out to do, begin by getting to know God and seeking His will in your life. If you do that, you *will* find Him. He *will* lead you. He *will* bless you. What a wonderful promise! But it is conditional. If you turn your back on the Lord, He will cast you off forever. I owe it to you, the reader, to emphasise that sobering warning as well.

How interesting it is that the young prince who heard his father's advice on that day went on to become perhaps the richest, most famous, and most glamorous king in the history of the world. He received twenty-five tons of gold every year (at today's value that is £465 million) and every form of wealth to go with it. The Scripture says,

'King Solomon was greater in riches and wisdom than all the other kings of the earth. All the kings of the earth sought audience with Solomon to hear the wisdom God had put in his heart. Year after year, everyone who came brought a gift—articles of silver and gold, and robes, weapons and spices, and horses and mules.

Solomon had four thousand stalls for horses and chariots, and twelve thousand horses, which he kept in the chariot cities and also with him in Jerusalem. He ruled over all the kings from the River to the land of the Philistines, as far as the border of Egypt. The king made silver as common in Jerusalem as stones, and cedar as plentiful as sycamore-fig trees in the foothills. Solomon's horses were imported from Egypt and from other countries' (2 Chronicles 9:22–31).

Whatever else you set out to do, begin by getting to know God and seeking His will in your life.

NOW, THAT'S POWER!

That, ladies and gentlemen, is known as *power!* Indeed, Solomon may have been the most powerful and respected man of all times. No good thing was withheld from him. For the purposes of our discussion, wouldn't it be helpful to know how he felt about the abundance he enjoyed? Well, fortunately, that information is available to us. Solomon wrote his innermost thoughts and recorded them in a book we know today as Ecclesiastes. The following excerpts are extremely important to understanding the point I have tried to make. Please read them carefully!

I undertook great projects: I built houses for myself and planted vineyards. I made gardens and parks and planted all kinds of fruit trees in them. I made reservoirs to water groves of flourishing trees. I bought male and female slaves and had other slaves who were born in my house. I owned more herds and flocks than anyone in Jerusalem before me. I amassed silver and gold for myself, and the treasure of kings and provinces. I acquired men and women singers, and a harem as well—the delights of the heart of man. I became greater by far than anyone in Jerusalem before me. In all this my wisdom stayed with me.

I denied myself nothing my eyes desired; I refused my heart no pleasure. My heart took delight in all my work, and this was the reward for all my labour. Yet when I surveyed all that my hands had done and what I had toiled to achieve, everything was meaningless, a chasing after the wind, nothing was gained under the sun. . . .

So I hated life, because the work that is done under the sun was grievous to me. All of it is meaningless, a chasing after the wind. I hated all the things I had toiled for under the sun, because I must leave them to the one who comes after me. And who knows whether he will be a wise man or a fool? Yet he will have control over all the work into which I have poured my effort and skill under the sun. This too is meaningless. (Ecclesiastes 2:4–11, 17–19)

What an incredible passage of Scripture this is, coming straight from the heart of an old man who had become disillusioned with life! It does not tell the entire story, however. Solomon failed to mention that he had strayed from the advice of his father and fell into grievous sin. God had specifically warned the children of Israel not to marry women from nations that worshipped idols and false gods. But Solomon willfully disobeyed this commandment and took hundreds of these foreigners to be his wives and concubines. The Scripture then tells where that defiance led.

As Solomon grew old, his wives turned his heart after other gods, and his heart was not fully devoted to the LORD his God, as the heart of David his father had been. He followed Ashtoreth the goddess of the Sidonians, and Molech the detestable god of the Ammonites. So Solomon did evil in the eyes of the LORD; he did not follow the LORD completely, as David his father had done. (1 Kings 11:4–6)

Now we know why Solomon was so depressed in the latter years of his life. He had a dark stain on his heart that was like a cancer gnawing at his insides. He had betrayed the God of his father, David. Can't you see the king bowing facedown before the false gods of Ashtoreth and Molech? These idols were used by pagan nations for the most unthinkable wickedness, including orgies and the sacrifice of innocent children. Yet Solomon, who had conversed with God and received every good gift from His hand, persisted in worshipping these evil symbols. Then he enticed the people of Israel to do likewise. Consequently, Solomon had lost all meaning in life, which explains his boredom with riches, fame, women, slaves, accomplishments, gold, and even laughter. God's hand was no longer on him.

The lesson for the rest of us is clear. If we ignore the Lord and violate His commandments, there will be no meaning for us, either. The temporal things of this world, even vast riches and power, will not deliver the satisfaction they advertise! There must be something more substantial on which to base one's values, purposes, and goals. And of course there is. Jesus said it succinctly: 'But seek ye *first* the kingdom of God, and his righteousness; and all these things shall be added unto you' (Matthew 6:33 KJV, emphasis mine).

I rest my case.

5

QUESTIONS FROM THE EDGE

Many of the topics presented in this book were originally discussed with 175 students in their late teens and early twenties who participated in a highly personal forum. For four days, I talked with these bright young men and women about the challenges associated with the 'critical decade'. Our purpose was to consider the important issues that arise during that era and to help young people retain their faith in a pagan world. Six video cameras and more than twenty microphones captured the event in vivid detail. The result was a spontaneous and stimulating discussion that has now been released to the public as a seven-part video series entitled (as this book), *Life on the Edge*.

Listed over are some of the edited questions and answers that occurred during the four-day interchange. Other items have been added to clarify and expand the concepts presented in this book. Incidentally, *your* comments and questions are welcome and will be considered for inclusion in future works on this subject. Send them to Dr James Dobson, Focus on the Family, Colorado Springs, Colorado 80995, USA. Appreciation is expressed to the Summit Ministry in Colorado Springs and its president, David Nobel, for bringing the students together for the video project. Our gratitude is also extended to the Navigators

Ministry in Colorado Springs for providing facilities for the taping sessions.

With that background, let's look at some questions and comments that relate to the ideas we have been discussing.

1. Your description of the 'Courtroom of the Mind' struck home with me. I have struggled with a poor self-image all my life, and I really don't know why. It just seems that everyone has more to offer than I do. I envy the guys who are better looking than I am, or they are more athletic or smarter. I just don't measure up to my own expectations. How can I deal with my own insecurities?

Someone said, 'Comparison is the root of all inferiority'. It is true. When you look at another person's strengths and compare them to your own weaknesses, there is no way to come out feeling good about yourself. That is what you are doing when you pit yourself against the 'best and brightest' around you. This destructive game begins in elementary school when we begin to evaluate ourselves critically. Even at that young age, our self-image is shaped by how we mea-

> *Mental and spiritual health begin with an acceptance of life as it is.*

sure up against our peers. It's not how tall we are that matters—it's who is tallest. It's not how fast we can run—it's who runs fastest. It's not how smart we are—it's who is smartest. It's not how pretty or handsome we are—it's who is most gorgeous. Thus begins a pattern of self-doubt that often becomes all-consuming during adolescence. Then it continues well into adult life. This is why millions of women buy fashion magazines and then envy the beauty of the models. It's why we watch beauty contests and why some men read about successful and powerful businessmen. When we do that, we're weighing ourselves against the assets of others. It is an exercise that brings us nothing but pain, and yet we continue to engage in it.

It appears that you are caught up in this destructive pattern. Perhaps a wise counsellor or pastor can help you see that you are a worthy human being exactly the way you are and that God has designed you for a specific purpose. Mental and spiritual health begin with an acceptance of life as it is and a willingness to make the most of what has been given. When that is achieved, comparison with others is no longer an important issue.

2. I have always been a good student, and I want to go to either law school or medical school. That means I could be in my mid- or late-twenties by the time I graduate and get on with life. But I also want to be a wife and mother and stay home with my children. I can't figure out how to achieve both these goals. How can I be a professional and a mother, too?

You've described a dilemma that millions of young women struggle with today. Three competing choices lie before them—whether to have a career, be a wife and mother, or attempt to do both. It is a decision that will have implications for everything that is to follow.

Since you don't yet have plans to get married, I would recommend that you press ahead with your academic goals. Once your training is complete, you will still have all the options available to you. If by that time you are married and want to become a full-time mother, you can put your career on hold for a few years or leave it altogether. Remember you can always return to it after the children are grown up. Or you can try to balance the two roles until the children are older.

Only you can decide what is best for yourself, of course. I

would strongly suggest that you make it a matter of prayer as you seek the Lord's will for your life.

3. Let me ask the question another way. Should a college-educated woman feel that she has wasted her training if she chooses not to use it professionally? I mean, why should I bother to go through school to be a professional if I'm going to end up raising children and being a full-time house-wife?

A person doesn't go to college just to prepare for a line of work—or at least, that shouldn't be the reason for being there. The purpose for getting a college education is to broaden your outlook and enrich your intellectual life. Whether or not it leads to a career is not the point. Nothing invested in the cultivation of your own mind is ever really wasted. If you have the desire to learn and the opportunity to go to school, I think you should reach for it. Your career plans can be finalised later.

4. Do you think it is alright for a woman to make it her exclusive career goal to be a wife and mother? Or should there be something else?

You bet it's all right! Motherhood is an honourable profession that didn't have to be defended for thousands of years. But in the last few decades, young women have been made to feel foolish if they even dared to mention that their goal was being a house-wife.

I remember a college senior who came to see me about her plans after graduation. We talked about various job opportunities and the possibility of her going to graduate school. Then she suddenly paused and looked over her shoulder. She leaned towards me and said almost in a whisper, 'May I be completely honest with you?'

I said, 'Sure, Debbie. There's nobody here but us. You can say anything you want.'

> *There is no more important job in the universe than to raise a child to love God.*

'Well,' she continued in a hushed tone, 'I don't want to have a career at all. What I really want is to be a full-time wife and mother.'

I said, 'Why do you say that like it's some kind of secret? It's your life. What's wrong with doing whatever you want with it?'

'Are you kidding?' she said. 'If my professors and my classmates at the university knew that's what I wanted, they'd laugh me out of school.'

Unbelievably, it has become politically incorrect to have babies and to devote time raising them. That is foolish and insulting. There is no more important job in the universe than to raise a child to love God, live productively, and serve humanity. How ridiculous that a woman should have to apologise for wanting to fulfill this historic role!

Not every woman chooses to be a wife and mother, of course. Some are interested only in a career. Others have no plans to marry. That is all right, too. But those who do elect to be full-time, stay-at-home mums should not be ashamed to admit it—even on a university campus.

5. You've talked about being a full-time mother versus having a full-time career. Give us your view of a woman handling both responsibilities simultaneously. Can it be done and is it smart?

Some women are able to maintain a busy career and a bustling home-life at the same time, and they do it beautifully. I admire them for their discipline and dedication. It has been my observation, however, that this dual responsibility is a formula for exhaustion and frustration for many others. It can be a never-ending struggle for survival. Why? Because there is only so much energy within the human body, and when it is invested in one place it is not available for use in another. Consider what it is like to be a mother of young children who must rise early in the morning, get her kids dressed, fed and located for the day, then drive to work, labour from nine to five, go by the supermarket and pick up some food for dinner, retrieve the children and then drive home. She is dog-tired by this point and needs to put her feet up for a few minutes. But she can't rest. The kids are hungry, and they've been waiting to see her all day.

'Read me a story, Mum,' says the most needy.

This beleaguered woman then begins another four to six hours of very demanding 'mothering' that will extend into the evening. She must prepare dinner, wash the dishes, bathe the baby, help with homework, and give each child some 'quality time'. Then comes the task of getting the 'tribe' into bed, saying prayers, and bringing glasses of water to giggling children who don't want to go to bed. I get tired just thinking about a schedule like this.

You might ask, 'Where is the husband and father in all this exertion? Why isn't he doing his share of the homework?' Well, he may be working a fifteen-hour day at his own job. Getting started in a business or a profession often demands that kind of commitment. Or he may simply not choose to help his wife. That is a common complaint among working mothers.

'Not fair,' you say.

I agree, but that's the way the system often works.

The most difficult aspect of this lifestyle is the constancy of the load. Most of us could maintain such a schedule for a week or two, but the working mother must do it month after month for years on end. On weekends, there's house-cleaning to do and clothes to be ironed and trousers to be mended. And this is the pace she maintains when things are going *right*. She has no reserve of time or energy when a member of the family becomes sick or the car breaks down or marital problems develop. A little push in any direction and she could go over the edge.

Admittedly, I have painted a more stressful scenario than most families have to endure. But not by much. Over-committed and exhausted families are commonplace in our culture. Husbands and wives have no time for each other. Life is nothing but work, work, work. They are continually frustrated, irritable, and harassed. They don't take walks together, read the Scriptures together, or do anything that is 'fun'. Their sex life suffers because exhausted people don't even make love meaningfully. They begin to drift apart and eventually find themselves with 'irreconcilable differences'. It is a tragic pattern I have been observing for the past twenty-five years.

The issue, then, is not whether a woman has a right to choose a career and be a mother, too. Of course she has that right, and it is nobody's business but hers and her husband's. I would simply plead that you don't allow your families to get sucked into that black hole of exhaustion. However you choose to divide the responsibilities of working and family management, reserve some time and energy for yourselves— and for each other. Your children deserve the best that you can give them, too.

6. My wife and I have only been married three years, and we already feel the pressures you are describing. We're trying to finish college, earn a living, and care for our little boy. It is too heavy a load. Where did we make our mistake?

Like many other people your age, you may be trying to do too much too soon. So many newly married couples try to go to school, have a child, buy and fix up a house, and be a two-career family at the same time. That is a recipe for trouble. The human body was not intended to be driven that hard. Something will break. Either physical illness will occur or relationships will flounder. I strongly suggest that you develop a more reasonable lifestyle even if it means lowering your expectations.

> *Overcommitted and exhausted families are commonplace in our culture.*

7. **How can we determine God's will for our lives? He doesn't speak to us in an audible voice. Do we just have to guess at what He wants?**

That is a very important question. You can't obey God if you are unclear about what He wants you to do. But most people lack a clear idea of how to discern His voice. They depend on feelings and impressions to interpret His will, which is unreliable and dangerous. What they feel is highly subjective. It is influenced by what they want, what is going on in their lives, and even how much sleep they got last night. Some terrible mistakes have been made by believers who thought they had heard the voice of the Lord.

I knew a college student who was awakened from a dream during the night with a strong impression that he should marry a certain young lady. They had dated only once or twice and hardly knew each other—yet 'God' had assured him that 'this is the one!' The next morning, he called the young woman and told her of his impression. The girl felt no such impulse, but didn't want to oppose a message directly from the Lord. The couple were married shortly thereafter and have suffered through the agonies of an unsuccessful and stormy marriage.

I could tell you many similar stories about people who misunderstood what seemed to have been the will of the Lord. Remember that Satan comes 'as an angel of light' (see 2 Corinthians 11:14), which means he counterfeits the voice of God. If he can get you to accept your impressions uncritically and impulsively, then he can confuse and disillusion you.

8. If you can't always trust what you feel, how can you know what is right?

There are at least five ways you can discern the will of the Lord. First, the apostle Paul wrote in the book of Ephesians, 'And this is my prayer. That . . . the God of our Lord Jesus Christ and the all-glorious Father, will give you spiritual wisdom and the insight to know more of him' (Ephesians 1:16 PHILLIPS). He wouldn't have said that unless it were possible through prayer to gain spiritual wisdom and insight. Therefore, a search for God's will should begin on your knees. He will meet you there. Remember that Jesus promised, 'Ask and it will be given to you; seek and you will find; knock and the door will be opened to you' (Matthew 7:7).

Second, you should examine the Scriptures for principles that relate to the issue at hand. The Lord will never ask you to do anything that is morally wrong or in contradiction to His Word. If what you are considering violates a concept you find in the Word, you can forget it.

Third, it is helpful to seek advice from those who are spiritually mature and solid in their faith. A godly counsellor or pastor can assist you in avoiding the common mistakes that confuse many young people.

Fourth, you should pay close attention to what is known as 'providential circumstances'. The Lord often speaks through doors that open or close. When you begin to be blocked on all sides in a particular pursuit, you might consider the possibility that God has other plans for you. I'm not suggesting that you give up at the first sign of obstacles but that you attempt to 'read' the events in your life for evidence of divine influence.

Fifth and finally, do *nothing* impulsively. Give God an opportunity to speak. Until He does, delay for a time and concentrate on the first four approaches.

By the way, these five steps are useful in finding the *specific* will of God, which each of us must discern for themselves. But I can tell you what His *general* will is. The Scripture gives all believers the same assignment, and it's called 'the Great Commission'. We find it in the words of Jesus, who said, 'Go ye into all the world, and preach the gospel to every creature' (Mark 16:15 KJV). That responsibility applies to all of us. Our task as believers is to tell as many people as possible that Jesus Christ died for our sins and offers eternal life to those who will believe in His name. So in whatever you do, whether you are a dentist, a truck-driver, an artist, a car dealer, or a housewife, you are expected to use that job to witness for the Saviour.

9. I believe God is calling me to be a youth minister when I get out of college, but I am concerned about how I can do that financially. Pastors don't make very much money, and if I have a family by then I'm not sure I could support them in that profession.

Let me share a very important spiritual principle that has been very helpful to me. We read in Psalm 119:105 that His Word is 'a lamp to my feet and a light for my path'. Think about the imagery described in that verse. We are not given a 300-watt beam to reveal the entire landscape. There is no headlight on our hats that points towards the horizon. Instead, the Lord provides only a hand-held lamp that illuminates the path on which we are walking. In other words, He shows us where to place the next step, and that is all. We have to trust Him to lead us through the darkness that lies beyond our vision.

There is an application here to your question. You're asking how the Lord is going to sustain you and your family in years to come. But the light you're carrying only shows what you need to know today. That is enough. Just continue to 'walk in the light' you have been given, and leave the future in God's hands. If He is calling you to do a job, He will make it possible for you to care for your family and overcome any other barriers to that responsibility.

10. I am like that person you described earlier. My rocket is on the launch pad but it isn't going anywhere. Frankly, I feel kind of lost and have no idea what to do next. How can I get my 'engines' to fire?

There are millions of young people who feel just like you do. That is, in fact, the primary reason I decided to write this book. As I said, it is very difficult today to get started in adult pursuits. There are no magic answers that will make everything fall into place, but I can offer two suggestions that others have found helpful.

First, career counsellors are equipped today with a battery of interest inventories, aptitude tests, and temperament scales that will help you get acquainted with yourself. It's worth the cost to seek out a specialist in this field and let them point you in the right direction. There are professions and positions that you probably don't know even exist. Talk to someone who does.

Second, find someone who is already working in a field

that you find interesting. Call or write to that person and ask if they will give you an hour or two of their time. A face-to-face meeting with a respected member of a profession or trade can tell you what you need to know.

That is precisely what I did when I was in my third year of college. My aunt went to hear a well-known Christian psychologist speak. Dr Clyde Narramore was that speaker, and he said, 'We need Christian young men and women in the field of mental health. If you know of promising students who are interested, I'll be glad to meet with them.' My aunt told me of this invitation, and I called Dr Narramore for an appointment. He graciously agreed to see me even though he was busy and 'didn't know me from Adam'. We spent two hours together in his living room during which he laid out a plan for how I could become a psychologist. It's been thirty-seven years since that conversation took place, and yet I still remember the advice he gave me that day. It shaped the next five years of my life and helped channel me into a profession I have loved.

Maybe there is a Clyde Narramore out there somewhere who might point you in the right direction. I hope so.

11. What do you think of placing children in childcare so mothers can work?

First, let me say that safe, clean, loving childcare facilities are a necessity in today's culture. They are especially needed by the millions of mothers who are forced to work for financial reasons. They are also vital to the many single parents who are the sole breadwinners in their families. Thus, we need not question the wisdom of providing well-supervised facilities for children whose mothers and fathers require assistance in raising them. That debate is over.

What can be argued is whether children get on better in a

childcare facility or at home with a full-time mum. Personally (and others will disagree) I don't believe any arrangement for children can compare with a whole family where the mother raises her children and the father is very involved in their lives.

First, they thrive and learn better when they enjoy one-to-one relationships with adults rather than as members of a group. Second, you can't pay an employee in childcare enough to care for children like their own mothers will do. Children are a mother's passion, and it shows. Third, research verifies that kids at home are healthier than those who are regularly exposed to diseases, coughs, and sneezes from other boys and girls.[1] Fourth, a bonding is more likely to occur between parents and children when the developmental milestones are experienced first-hand. Families should be there when the first step is taken, and the first word is spoken and when fears and anxieties arise. Certainly, others can substitute for Mum in those special moments, but something precious is lost if a surrogate witnesses them.

Finally, careful investigations of child development have yielded unequivocal results. One of the most ambitious studies was called the Harvard University Preschool Project, which was conducted by Dr Burton L. White and a team of fifteen researchers. They studied young children over a ten-year period in an effort to learn which experiences in the early years of life contribute to the development of healthy, intelligent human beings. Their conclusions are summarised below:

a. It is increasingly clear that the origins of human competence are to be found in a critical period of development between eight and eighteen months of age. The child's experiences during these brief months do more to influence future intellectual competence than any time before or after.

b. The single most important environmental factor in the life of the child is its mother. 'She is on the hook,' said Dr White, and carries more influence on her child's experiences than any other person or circumstance.

> *I don't believe any arrangement for children can compare with a whole family . . .*

c. The amount of 'live language' directed to a child (not to be confused with television, radio, or overheard conversations) is vital to its development of fundamental linguistic, intellectual, and social skills. The researchers concluded, 'providing a rich social life for a twelve- to fifteen-month-old child is the best thing you can do to guarantee a good mind.'

d. Those children who were given free access to living areas of their homes progressed much faster than those whose movements were restricted.

e. The nuclear family is the most important educational delivery system. If we are going to produce capable, healthy children, it will be by strengthening family units and by improving the interactions that occur within them.

f. The best parents were those who excelled at three key functions:

*   They were superb designers and organisers of their children's environments.

*   They permitted their children to interrupt them for

brief, thirty-second episodes, during which personal consultation, comfort, information, and enthusiasm were exchanged.

* They were firm disciplinarians while simultaneously showing great affection for their children.[2]

Occasionally, information comes along that needs to be filed away for future reference. These findings from the Harvard University Preschool Project are that important. Those of my readers who hope to have children someday, and those who have already produced them, will not want to forget these six items. I believe they hold the key to raising healthy children.

Can the findings from Dr White's study be applied by parents whose children are placed in childcare centres? Yes, and many of them do. It is just more difficult and challenging when an employee substitutes for a mother and father during the prime-time hours of the day.

12. If parents have to use childcare support, what kind of help do you think is best?

State-run facilities rank at the bottom of my list because Christian teaching is not permissible in private facilities. Children are not led in prayer before meals, and no reference can be made to God as our friend and Lord. I also worry more about the possibility of child molestation in state centres, even though it is rare. For these and other reasons, I prefer church-run programmes that are clean and safe. Even better, if available, is placement of children with relatives such as grandparents or aunts or supervision provided by other mothers. Children need to develop relationships with those who care for them. They should be left with adults they know and love, if possible, rather than relating to different employees from day to day in private facilities.

13. (Asked with great emotion) It is my desire . . . to follow Jesus Christ in everything I do. But I have no idea . . . what He wants of me or what I'm supposed to do. Is it enough that I'm willing?

We are told in the Scriptures that God is infinitely loving and compassionate towards us, His children. Psalm 103:13 says, 'As a father pities his children, so the Lord pities those who fear him' (NKJV). Isaiah 66:13 says, 'As a mother comforts her child, so will I comfort you.' Given those descriptions of God as the ultimate parent, can you imagine Him ignoring your request for direction and guidance in your life? Is there even a possibility that He would say, 'I don't care about her. She wants to do My will, but I'm going to conceal it from her. I'll just let her flounder'?

Not a chance! He sees those tears in your eyes. He knows the desire of your heart. And you *will* hear from Him—just in time to take the next step.

6

THE KEYS TO
LIFELONG LOVE

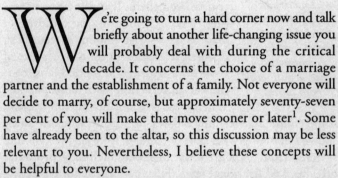

W e're going to turn a hard corner now and talk briefly about another life-changing issue you will probably deal with during the critical decade. It concerns the choice of a marriage partner and the establishment of a family. Not everyone will decide to marry, of course, but approximately seventy-seven per cent of you will make that move sooner or later[1]. Some have already been to the altar, so this discussion may be less relevant to you. Nevertheless, I believe these concepts will be helpful to everyone.

The tragedy of modern families is how frequently they break up. No one knows for sure what the probabilities of divorce are, but they are far too high. (We often hear that fifty per cent of marriages end in divorce, but that estimate is based on faulty information.) What we do know for certain is that marriage is a risky enterprise that must be entered into with great care. It can result either in lifelong companionship or some of the most bitter experiences in living.

Make no mistake about it, divorce can inflict terrible pain on its victims. Every member of the family suffers when a marriage breaks up. A Russian woman who was my guest on the radio talked about her years in a Nazi extermination camp. She had seen mass murder and every form of deprivation. After the war, she came to America and married, only to have her husband be unfaithful and abandon her a few years later. Unbelievably, she said that experience of rejection and loss was actually more painful than her years in a German death camp. That says it all.[2]

If husbands and wives suffer dramatically from the break-up of their families, imagine how much more painful it is for their vulnerable children. Some of you have reason to under-stand precisely what I mean because you've been there. It is not a pretty pic-ture. Research focusing on children of divorce shows that emotional security in children is dependent on the presence of a warm, nurturing, sustained, and con-tinuous interaction with *both* parents.

> *Emotional security in children is dependent on . . . continuous interaction with both parents.*

When these relationships are interrupted, some children never fully recover from it. In fact, one study showed that ninety per cent of children from divorced homes suffered from an acute sense of shock, including profound grieving and irrational fears. Fifty per cent reported feeling rejected and abandoned, and for good reason. Half the fathers stopped seeing their children approximately three-years after the divorce. Most significantly, thirty seven per cent of the children were even more unhappy and dissatisfied five years after the divorce than they had been at eighteen months. In other words, time did not heal their wounds.[3]

IT'S CHILDREN WHO SUFFER MOST

These hurting children are all around us. I remember wait-ing to catch a plane at Los Angeles International Airport a few years ago, engaging in my favourite activity of people-watching. Standing near me was an old man who was ob-viously waiting for someone who should have been on the plane that arrived minutes before. He examined each face intently as the passengers filed past. I thought he seemed upset as he waited.

Then I saw a little girl who stood by his side. She must have been seven years old, and she, too, was looking intently for a certain face in the crowd. I have rarely seen a child more anxious than this little girl. She clung to the old man's arm, whom I assumed to be her grandfather. Then as the last passengers came by, one by one, the girl began to cry silently. She was not merely disappointed at that moment; her little heart was broken. The grandfather also appeared to be fighting back the tears. In fact, he was too upset to comfort the child, who then buried her face in the sleeve of his worn coat.

'Oh, God!' I prayed silently. 'What special agony are they experiencing in this hour? Was it the child's mother who abandoned her on that painful day? Did her daddy promise to come and then change his mind?'

My impulse was to hug the little girl and shield her from the disappointment of that moment. I wanted to let her pour out her grief in the protection of my arms, but I feared that my intrusion would be misunderstood. So I watched helplessly. The old man and the child stood silently as the passengers departed from two other planes. Then the anxiety on their faces turned to despair. Finally, they walked slowly through the terminal and towards the door as the little girl fought to control her tears.

Where is that child now? God only knows. Perhaps she will read this book someday and drop me a line. I hope so. And I pray that the pieces of her broken world will come back together. But there are millions of other children in other places who have gone through similar circumstances. Permit me one more illustration.

The following letter was published in *American Girl*

magazine some years ago. A fourteen-year-old girl named Vicki Kraushaar had submitted it for publication in the section of the magazine entitled, 'By You'. This is what she wrote:

THAT'S THE WAY LIFE GOES SOMETIMES

When I was ten, my parents got a divorce. Naturally, my father told me about it, because he was my favourite. [Notice that Vicki did not say, 'I was *his* favourite'.]

'Honey, I know it's been kind of bad for you these past few days, and I don't want to make it worse. But there's something I have to tell you. Honey, your mother and I got a divorce.'

'But Daddy—'

'I know you don't want this, but it has to be done. Your mother and I just don't get along like we used to. I'm already packed and my plane is leaving in half an hour.'

'But, Daddy, why do you have to leave?'

'Well, honey, your mother and I can't live together anymore.'

'I know that, but I mean why do you have to leave town?'

'Oh. Well, I got someone waiting for me in New Jersey.'

'But, Daddy, will I ever see you again?'

'Sure you will, honey. We'll work something out.'

'But what? I mean, you'll be living in New Jersey, and I'll be living here in Washington.'

'Maybe your mother will agree to you spending two weeks in the summer and two in the winter with me.'

'Why not more often?'

'I don't think she'll agree to two weeks in the summer and two in the winter, much less more.'

'Well, it can't hurt to try.'

'I know, honey, but we'll have to work it out later. My plane leaves in twenty minutes and I've got to get to the airport. Now I'm going to get my luggage, and I want you to go to your room so you don't have to watch me. And no long good-byes either.'

'OK, Daddy. Good-bye. Don't forget to write.'

'I won't. Good-bye. Now go to your room.'

'OK. Daddy, I don't want you to go!'

'I know, honey. But I have to.'

'Why?'

'You wouldn't understand.'

'Yes I would.'

'No, you wouldn't.'

'Oh well. Good-bye.'

'Good-bye. Now go to your room. Hurry up.'

'OK. Well, I guess that's the way life goes sometimes.'

'Yes, honey. That's the way life goes sometimes.'

After my father walked out that door, I never heard from him again.[4]

I'm so sorry, Vicki, that you had to go through this heartache at such a young age. Thank you for sharing your pain with us. Maybe it will help others avoid the errors of your parents. If we can prevent just one marriage from disintegrating—or just one child from suffering the loss of a family—our effort will be justified.

FOR THOSE OF YOU WHO PLAN TO MARRY

To my readers who plan to marry, I urge you to be extremely careful in the selection of a mate. Bathe the matter in prayer, and bring all of your intelligence to bear on this decision. You do not want the tragedy of divorce to happen to you. It *must not* happen to you.

Unfortunately, many young people are not so cautious. They move glibly through their courtship and into marriage, not seeming to realise just how much is at stake for them. They remind me of a chocolate lover peering into a box of delicious chocolates. They have been offered only one piece, and the decision is killing them. There are too many choices. Some are creams, some contain nuts, some are fruit-filled, and some are chewy nougats. Their mouth waters for a particular chocolate, but where is it? In frustration, they begin crushing the tops to see what's inside of them. Finally, they bite into the one they have chosen. If they make a mistake, they will know it instantly. But by then, it is too late. The box is passed to someone else.

> *I urge you to be extremely careful in the selection of a mate.*

Haven't you seen young men and women looking intently for the 'perfect' chocolate? They know what they want, but aren't sure how to find it. Furthermore, the decoration on the outside is often misleading. Their search leads them to crush many potential lovers along the way. At last, they 'bite' into the chosen delicacy, only to realise very quickly that they should have given the matter a little more thought.

The important question is, How will you select the right chocolate from all the alternatives? How will you avoid a sour surprise after it is too late to reconsider? How will you beat the odds against a successful marriage? How will you prevent the fever of infatuation from turning into a marital rash? What are the principles that support a relationship and give it the best chance of growing and maturing and surviving?

Those questions have been examined carefully by a researcher named Desmond Morris.[5] His findings should be very enlightening to you. Dr Morris wanted to understand why some couples develop a mystical union that holds them together for a lifetime while others fall apart when the pressure is on. The investigation began.

Dr Morris soon recognised that the difference between

successful and unsuccessful marriages can often be traced to how well couples are able to 'bond' during the courtship period. By bonding he referred to the process by which a man and woman become cemented together emotionally. It describes the chemistry that permits two previous strangers to become intensely valuable to one another. It helps them weather the storms of life and remain committed in sickness and health, for richer or poorer, for better or worse, forsaking all others until they are parted in death. It is a phenomenal experience that almost defies description.

SOMEONE ON YOUR TEAM

Instead of being alone, a person's basic need for love, belonging, and acceptance is met in that precious relationship. If it has happened to you, there is now someone on your team who is looking out for your welfare. This person is fighting for you and defending you and praying for you. It's someone who will be there when things go wrong. He or she will also share your hopes and dreams and joy. And if your union should be blessed with children, this person will help you raise them in the fear and admonition of the Lord.

This special bonding is God's gift of companionship to the human family. It all started in the Garden of Eden when the first man, Adam, showed evidence of great loneliness. Can't you see him sitting on a log in the middle of the garden, drawing little circles in the sand with his toe? His eyes are glassy, and he yawns absent-mindedly. The Creator looks at Adam compassionately and says, 'It is not good for the man to be alone' (Genesis 2:19). Imagine that! Even though Adam could fellowship with God Himself in the cool of the day, he needed something else. He needed human companionship. So the Father said, 'I will make a helper suitable for him' (Genesis 2:18).

That word *suitable* in this scripture is one of the Lord's profound understatements! He beautifully designed the sexes for one another, giving each gender the precise characteristics needed by the other. Consider, for example, how men and women's bodies were crafted to 'fit' together sexually. Anyone, even the most avid evolutionist, can see that they were constructed anatomically for one another. In the same way, the emotional apparatus of males and females is designed to interlock. It fits like hand in glove. Having thus prepared us lovingly for one another, the Lord revealed His plan for the family: ' "For this reason a man will leave his father and mother and be united to his wife, and the two will become one flesh." So they are no longer two, but one. Therefore what God has joined together, let man not separate' (Mark 10:7–9).

That is the way the system was designed. Unfortunately, there is a flaw in its implementation. Sin has invaded God's creation, and we now live in a fallen world. God's beautiful plan has been corrupted by selfishness, lust, greed, jealousy, suspicion, adultery, immaturity and other distortions of the human personality. Consequently, romantic love sometimes fails to deliver on its promise, even among God-fearing people. Someone observed, 'Marriages are made in heaven, but so are lightning and thunder.'

WILL YOU EXPERIENCE
TRUE INTIMACY?

Studies have shown that only ten per cent of couples ever experience true intimacy in their relationship. Others may remain together for the sake of the children or from a sense of duty or because they genuinely care about each other. But they never achieve the companionship and affection they desire and need.

In that kind of imperfect world, let me ask you again about your own future. How will you secure the prize of intimacy in marriage? What are the keys to a deeply committed and satisfying relationship? How will you go the distance when others within your generation are breaking up every day? Is there a way to improve your prospects for marital happiness?

> *Romantic love sometimes fails to deliver on its promise.*

For the answers, let's review the findings of Dr Morris. He said the quality of the bond made during courtship is the key to successful marriages. Then he explained how that cementing process occurs. Dr Morris believes, and I strongly agree, that couples are most likely to bond securely when they have not rushed the dating experience. Time is the critical ingredient.

That reminds me of my efforts to build model aeroplanes when I was a boy. In those days, one could buy inexpensive kits that included a sheet of balsa wood on which the parts of the model had been stamped. It was a big chore to cut them out with a craft knife and then glue all the pieces together. Once that was finished, tissue paper was pasted to the frame. The final result was a beautiful little plane to hang in your bedroom. I wanted to build one of those models in the worst way, but I never got it done. Repeatedly, I bought a kit and began cutting out the pieces. But I couldn't finish the project because I was too impatient to wait for the glue to dry. I wouldn't leave the fuselage alone, and it would fall apart in my hands.

That's more or less what Dr Morris has told us about romantic relationships. It takes time for the glue to dry. A proper bond between two people is severely damaged if the process is rushed. Specifically, he said there are twelve stages of intimacy through which couples should progress if they want to develop a permanent commitment to each other.

These stages begin with the most casual contact and move through categories of increasing familiarity. Let's look at them individually.

The quality of the bond made during courtship is the key to successful marriages.

Stage one is called **Eye-to-Body**. It is the least intimate of all contacts between two people. All that has occurred so far is that one person has seen another. They don't know each other and have no relationship whatsoever. But every worthwhile venture has to start somewhere. If there is an attraction between them, they will build on that moment of recognition.

Stage two is called **Eye-to-Eye**. This refers to the first time they look directly at one another. An electrochemical spark crackles somewhere in the brain, and a little voice says, 'Hey, Man! Pay attention! This could be interesting!'

I remember when that moment first occurred between me and the woman who is now my wife. Shirley and I were students at the same college although we had never met. Our paths finally crossed one day while I was eating lunch with some friends. Suddenly, I saw this girl sitting on the other side of the cafeteria. *Man!* I said to myself. *That girl is pretty.*

I kept looking at her, and soon she realised she was being watched. Shirley glanced at me and smiled seductively. I smiled back. I took another bite and then checked to see if she was looking at me. She was. In a few minutes she looked to see if I was looking at her. I was. The charade went on throughout lunchtime. I don't remember what I ate that day, but it was one of the most exciting meals of the year.

Still, I knew nothing about the student in the cafeteria. I couldn't have told you her name or anything about her. We had not even talked at that point. Our entire relationship was confined to a series of glances and flirtatious smiles. Then we went our separate ways. This encounter is rather typical for two people in the eye-to-eye stage of relation-ships. For some, that's the end of the story. For Shirley and me, it prefaced a lifetime of love and friendship.

Stage three is called **Voice-to-Voice**. It involves the first conversation between two potential romantic partners. Their words are usually tentative and uncomfortable at that point, involving brilliant questions such as, 'What's your name?' and 'Isn't this a neat day?' For Shirley and me, however, the first interchange was a bit more cre-ative.

> *She walked past me and said with a smile, 'Hello, Legs!'*

Shortly after our 'look-a-thon' in the cafeteria, I was standing near the campus tennis courts where I spent much of my time. Hundreds of students were moving between classes, and among them was this pretty lady I had been admiring. I saw her coming my way and began thinking about what I would say to her. She was doing some thinking too. Remembering that I often wore white tennis shorts, she walked past me and said with a smile, 'Hello, Legs!'

The little flirt got my attention, I promise you that! Anyone who likes my legs can't be all bad. I was so surprised by her remark, however, that I don't recall saying anything in return. I certainly thought about it for several days. That was our first 'conversation', consisting of two flirtatious words uttered in stage three, voice-to-voice.

A week later, another interesting interchange took place. I saw Shirley standing with a group of friends near her dor-mitory. I walked up and engaged her in small talk. Then I took a coin out of my pocket and started flipping it in the air.

I said, 'I have a remarkable ability that you ought to know about. I can call the toss of a coin—heads or tails—with unbelievable accuracy. I never miss.'

Shirley took the bait. 'Let me see you do it,' she said.

'All right, but it's gonna cost you.' I replied. 'I will flip this coin in the air, and I'll bet you a hamburger I can tell you whether it falls heads or tails.'

It was what is known as a 'sure thing'. If I won, I would get to take Shirley out for a hamburger. If I lost, she would buy one for me. I would be the winner either way. So I tossed the coin and accurately called it heads.

'OK,' I asked, 'when are you going to buy?'

'Not so fast,' replied Shirley. 'Let's go double or nothing.'

'Fair enough,' I said, and tossed the coin again. Once more, I called accurately.

'Double or nothing again,' she demanded.

Up went the coin, and unbelievably, I was three for three. Shirley then owed me four hamburgers.

'I can't stop now,' she said. 'Toss it again.'

We played that ridiculous game for several minutes, during which I never missed a call. By the time we were finished, Shirley owed me sixty-four hamburgers, and she's been frying them ever since. That was the beginning of a lifetime of conversation that continues to this day.

Stage four is called **Hand-to-Hand**, and it is slightly more personal and intimate than anything that has gone before. At this early point, holding the hand of a potential romantic partner can be exciting. It doesn't represent familiarity or a commitment, but it does indicate that the friendship is progressing. A person would not approach a total stranger on the street and ask to hold their hand. Why not? Because that act is reserved for those who have developed at least a certain affection for one another.

You may be too young to remember an enormously popular recording by a rock group known as The Beatles. It was one of their early sensational hits and was titled, *I Wanna Hold Your Hand*. The entire song focused on the thrill of holding hands. One might wonder about The Beatles getting so shook up over something so ordinary. But anyone who has ever been in love will understand their sentiment very well.

Stage five is called **Hand-to-Shoulder,** which is slightly more personal than the holding of hands. It reflects a 'buddy' type of relationship where the partners are still side by side rather that facing each other. At this stage of intimacy, a hand to the shoulder indicates more of a friendship than an expression of commitment.

Stage six is called **Hand-to-Waist.** This position is clearly more romantic than any of the prior stages. Casual friends do not stand and embrace each other in that way. It is just one more stop along the way to a deeper, more intimate relationship.

Stage seven is called **Face-to-Face.** This level of contact involves gazing into one another's eyes, hugging, and kissing. If the previous stages have not been rushed, it has meaning beyond anything that has gone before. Typically, it is a reflection of sexual desire and romantic feelings between the partners.

Of course, many people engage in face-to-face activity that is merely frivolous and titillating. I was once counted among them. I got my first kiss when I was thirteen years of age. I was with an 'older woman' of fifteen who took advantage of my innocence. Just as I used a coin to get Shirley's attention, this girl used one to play a trick on me. She bet five cents that she could kiss me without touching me.

'That's impossible!' I said.

'Try me,' said the girl.

'You have a deal,' I said.

This young lady then kissed me good and handed me the coin. 'You win,' she said.

I loved it! Maybe that's how I came up with the

hamburger proposition offered to Shirley eight years later. I wish I could say the same coin was used in both situations. That would make a great story, but it isn't true. It is accurate to say that there are two lucky five cent pieces out there somewhere that figured significantly in my development as a great lover.

Stage eight is called **Hand-to-Head.** Surprisingly, touching a person's hair in a romantic way is more intimate than kissing and nuzzling face-to-face. Stroking the head is simply not done by strangers or even casual friends in this culture.

I was sitting in church one morning and watching a toddler in front of me who was cradled on his mother's lap. He was sucking his thumb and gently caressing his mum's curls with his other hand. This mother showed no signs of objecting to her baby's familiarity with her hair. As I watched this display of affection, I considered with amusement the possibility of doing the same thing. I wouldn't have done it, of course, but it was interesting to speculate. If I had leaned forward and wound a curly lock around my finger, Mum might have hit me with a hymnal. Why? Because I would have made an intimate gesture that our relationship did not warrant. I elected not to touch the lady.

Touching a person's hair in a romantic way is more intimate than kissing and muzzling face to face.

Stages nine through twelve are distinctly sexual and private. They are **Hand-to-Body, Mouth-to-Breast, Touching below the Waist,** and **Sexual Intercourse.** Obviously, these acts of physical intimacy should be reserved exclusively for the marriage bed. They were intended to be enjoyed by two people who have pledged themselves to lifelong love and irrevocable commitment.

MARITAL BONDING: IT TAKES TIME

Now let's draw the greater meaning from these stages of marital bonding as outlined for us by Dr Desmond Morris. As we've indicated, he emphasised the necessity of moving slowly and methodically through the various steps. Furthermore, it is important, he said, not to skip any of them. In other words, they should be taken in sequence. Singer Frank Sinatra recorded a song years ago that included this line, 'Let's take it nice and easy, making all the stops along the way.'[6] That's the basic idea.

Bonding is damaged when couples scramble the stages. If they kiss passionately on the first date, engage in heavy petting a month later, or have sexual intercourse before marriage, something precious is lost in their commitment to one another. They have not allowed the 'glue' to dry. Unfortunately, that's how the entertainment industry presents the ideal romantic relationship. A young man and woman are shown being introduced, and the next thing you know, they're making passionate love together. According to Dr Morris, that exploitation for momentary pleasure carries serious implications for the future of the relationship.

When the various stages are taken slowly and in order, two people have a chance to become knowledgeable of each other on an emotional, as opposed to a physical, level. Their courtship is nurtured through leisurely walks and talks and 'lover's secrets' that lay a foundation for mutual intimacy. They talk endlessly about anything and everything. And by the time they marry, there is very little they don't know about each other. Romantic commitments are born in those prolonged conversations.

At the risk of trivialising a beautiful concept, let me share the words of an old country song that illustrates this verbal intimacy. Though the lyrics were apparently intended to be

humorous, they speak clearly about the voice-to-voice stage
of courtship from which bonded relationships develop. This
is 'corny' stuff, but I like it anyway.

> I'm the official historian on Shirley Jean Burrell.
> I've known her since Lord only knows and I won't tell;
> I caught her the first time she stumbled and fell,
> And Shirley, she knows me just as well.
> I can tell you her birthday and her daddy's middle name,
> The uncles on her momma's side and ones they don't claim;
> What she's got for Christmas since nineteen fifty-two
> And that's only the beginning of the things I could tell you.
>
> I can tell you her fav'rite song and where she'd like to park,
> And why to this very day she's scared of the dark;
> How she got her nickname and the scar behind her knee,
> If there's anything you need to know 'bout Shirley, just ask
>   me.
> I know where she's ticklish and her every little quirk,
> The funnies she don't read, and her number at work;
> I know what she stands for and what she won't allow.
> The only thing that I don't know is where, where she is right
>   now.[7]

It appears that Shirley Jean Burrell and her singing
boyfriend are well on their way to a bonded relationship. I
do hope they will be happy together.

Before we tuck away this understanding of bonded commitments, let me emphasise that the concept applies not
only to the courtship period. The most successful marriages
are those in which husbands and wives stroll through the
twelve steps regularly in their daily lives. Nor does the need
for that interaction go away as the years unfold. Touching
and talking and holding hands and gazing into one another's eyes, and building memories are as important to
partners in their midlife years as to those in the critical

decade. Indeed, the best way to invigorate a tired sex life is to walk through the twelve steps of courtship—regularly and with gusto!

Here is one more little tip that I hope my male readers will salt away for future reference: Women resent being rushed through stages ten, eleven, and twelve, when their husbands haven't taken the time for the previous nine. They often feel 'used' under those circumstances.

Tina Turner recorded a hit song a few years ago that asked the question, 'What's love got to do with it?'[8] That is what is communicated when physical intimacy is expected in the absence of romance. It's as though love is irrelevant, and this attitude reduces the mystical union of intercourse to an animalistic act. If you want to have an energised sex life in marriage, try a little tenderness during the other twenty-three and a half hours of the day. Remember, you read it here.

SUGGESTIONS TO HELP YOU FIND LIFE-LONG LOVE

Well, let's bring this discussion in for a landing with a few other 'keys to lifelong love'. I could write a book on this subject—in fact I already have. It's called *Love for a Lifetime,* and might be helpful to those who are contemplating marriage or are already newlyweds. At this point, I'll leave you with five straightforward recommendations:

1. A Sunday school teacher gave me some advice when I was thirteen years of age that I never forgot. He said, 'Don't marry the person you think you can live with. Marry the one you can't live without.' There's great truth in this advice. Marriage can be difficult even when two people are passionately in love with one another. It is murder when they don't have that foundation to build on.

2. Don't marry someone who has characteristics that you feel are intolerable. You may plan to change them in the future, but that probably won't happen. Behaviour runs in deep channels that were cut during early childhood, and it is very difficult to alter them. In order to change a deeply ingrained pattern, you have to build a sturdy dam, dig another canal, and reroute the river in a new direction. That effort is rarely successful over the long term.

Therefore, if you can't live with a characteristic that shows up during courtship, it may plague you for the rest of your life. For example, a person who drinks every night is not likely to give up that habit after the honeymoon. If they are foolish with money or basically unclean or tend to become violent when irritated or are extremely selfish, these are red flags you should not ignore. What you see is what you get.

Of course, we all have flaws, and I'm not suggesting that a person has to be perfect to be a candidate for marriage. Rather, my point is that you have to decide if you can tolerate a quirky behaviour for the rest of your life—because that's how long you may have to deal with it. If you can't, don't bank on deprogramming the partner after you've said 'I do.' I advise you to keep your eyes wide open before marriage and then half-closed thereafter.

3. Do not marry impulsively! I can think of no better way to mess up your life than to leap into this critical decision without careful thought and prayer. It takes time to get acquainted and to walk through the first eight steps of the bonding process. Remember that the dating relationship is designed to conceal information, not reveal it. Both partners put on their best faces for the one they seek to attract. They guard the secrets that might be a turn-off. Therefore, many newlyweds get a big surprise during the

first year of married life. I suggest that you take at least a year to get beyond the façade and into the inner character of the person.

4. If you are a deeply committed Christian, do not allow yourself to become 'unequally yoked' with an unbeliever. You may expect to win your spouse over to the Lord at some future date, and that does happen on occasion. But to count on it is risky at best, foolhardy at worst.

> *Don't marry someone who has characteristics that you feel are intolerable.*

Again, this is the question that must be answered: 'Just how critical is it that my husband (or wife) shares my faith?' If it is essential and non-negotiable, as the Scripture tells us it should be for believers, then this matter should be given the highest priority in one's decision to marry.

5. Do not move in with a person before marriage. To do so is a bad idea for many reasons. First, it is immoral and a violation of God's law. Second, it undermines a relationship and often leads to divorce. Studies show that couples who live together before marriage have a fifty per cent greater chance of divorce than those who don't, based on fifty years of data.[9] Those who cohabit also have less satisfying and more unstable marriages. Why? The researchers found those who had lived together later regretted having 'violated their moral standards', and 'felt a loss of personal freedom to exit out the back door'. Furthermore, and in keeping with the theme of marital bonding, they have 'stolen' a level of intimacy that is not warranted at that point, nor has it been validated by the degree of commitment to one another. As it turns out, God's way is not only the right way—it is the healthiest for everyone concerned.

6. Don't get married too young. Those who wed between the ages of fourteen and seventeen are twice as likely to divorce as couples who wait until their twenties. Making it as a family requires some characteristics that come with maturity, such as selflessness, stability, and self-control. It's best to wait for their arrival.

7. Finally, I'll conclude with the ultimate secret of lifelong love. Simply put, the stability of marriage is a by-product of an iron-willed determination to make it work. If you choose to marry, enter into that covenant with the resolve to remain committed to each other for life. Never threaten to leave your partner during angry moments. Don't allow yourself to consider even the possibility of divorce. Calling it quits must not become an option for those who want to go the distance!

That was the attitude of my father when he married my mother in 1935. Forty years later, he and I were walking in a park and talking about the meaning of commitment between a husband and wife. With that, he reached in his pocket and took out a worn piece of paper. On it was written a promise he had made to my mother when she agreed to become his wife. This is what he had said to her:

I want you to understand and be fully aware of my feelings concerning the marriage covenant which we are about to enter. I have been taught at my mother's knee, and in harmony with the Word of God, that the marriage vows are inviolable, and by entering into them I am binding myself absolutely and for life. The idea of estrangement from you through divorce for any reason at all (although God allows one—infidelity) will never at any time be permitted to enter into my thinking. I'm not naïve in this. On the contrary, I'm fully aware of the possibility, unlikely as it now appears, that mutual incompatibility or other unforeseen circumstances could result in extreme mental suffering. If such becomes the case, I am resolved for my part to accept it as a consequence of the commitment I am now making, and to bear it, if necessary, to the end of our lives together.

I have loved you dearly as a sweetheart and will continue to love you as my wife. But over and above that, I love you with a Christian love that demands that I never react in any way towards you that would jeopardise our prospects of entering heaven, which is the supreme objective of both our lives. And I pray that God Himself will make our affection for one another perfect and eternal.

If that is the way you approach the commitment of marriage, your probabilities of living happily together are vastly improved. Again, the Scripture endorses the permanence of the marital relationship: 'Therefore what God has joined together, let man not separate' (Mark 10:9).

> *The stability of marriage is a by-product of an iron-willed determination to make it work.*

7

LOVE MUST
BE TOUGH

I want to describe a principle now that could be useful to you for the rest of your life. It concerns how people relate to each other and the forces that draw them together. It also explains what drives them apart. Although our focus here will be on romantic relationships, this concept applies wherever human interests intersect, including employees and employers, friends and neighbours, or daughters and mothers-in-law.

To explain this principle, which I described more completely in my book *Love Must Be Tough,* let me ask you to recall an occasion when you believed you had fallen madly in love with someone in your school. You thought about that person night and day and fantasised about how wonderful and exciting they were. You plotted and schemed to make yourself attractive and interesting. Eventually, you got your wish, and the object of your obsession began to like you, too.

Not only did that individual return your affection, but in time, they began to chase you and demand your attention. Instead of hoping and dreaming that you might be loved in return, you quickly began to feel pressed—trapped—claustrophobic. The more you back-pedalled, the more aggressive this individual became. You wanted to escape and could hardly tolerate that person you once thought you couldn't live without.

That's the way we are made, emotionally. Most of us want what we have to stretch for—what we can only dream about achieving. We are excited by a challenge—by that which is mysterious and elusive. It's called 'the lure of the unattainable', and it is a powerful force in our lives. Conversely, we don't want the doormat we can't get rid of.

Mutual respect is critical. The exciting chemistry that sometimes develops between a man and a woman depends on the perception that each is fortunate to have attracted the other. The moment one begins to build a cage around the other and to proclaim, 'I own you,' the game is over. Let me illustrate.

MY COURTSHIP DAYS

When I first met my wife, Shirley, she was a lowly second year student in college and I was a lofty senior. I viewed myself as a big man on campus, and I wasn't very enthusiastic about the 'new kid on the block'. But she felt very differently. She had been very successful with boys and was challenged by the independence she saw in me. She wanted

Mutual respect is critical.

to win me because she wasn't sure she could. I understood that and held our friendship very loosely.

After my graduation, Shirley and I had one of those tension-filled conversations known to lovers the world over. I said I wanted her to date other guys while I was in the army because I didn't plan to get married soon. I liked her a lot, but I just didn't think I loved her. We could still be friends in the future, but the relationship was basically over.

It was a bombshell for which Shirley had no preparation. She hadn't seen it coming. We had been dating for more than a year and had built many warm memories together. That's why I thought she would be devastated. Although I didn't want to hurt her, I fully expected her to cry and hold on to me. Instead, Shirley said quietly and confidently, 'I've been thinking the same thoughts and I *would* like to date other guys. Why don't we just go our separate ways for now?'

Her answer rocked me. Was she really going to let me go without a struggle? I walked her to her dorm and asked if I could kiss her good-bye. She said, 'No,' and went inside. Who would have believed it?

What I didn't learn for many months was that Shirley went up to her room, closed the door, and cried all night. But she knew intuitively that she could not let me see her pain. She let me go with such dignity and respect that I immediately began wondering if I had done the right thing. I had been hoping to escape gracefully, but now I questioned whether I really wanted to go. The next day I wrote her a letter and apologised, asking to continue the relationship. Shirley waited two weeks to answer.

I went away to the army and later returned to the University of Southern California to begin my graduate training. By this time, Shirley was an exalted senior and I was a collegiate has-been. She was homecoming queen, senior class president, a member of *Who's Who in American Colleges and Universities,* and one of the most popular girls in her class. And I have to tell you, she began to look very good to me. I began calling her several times a day, complaining about who she was spending her time with and trying to find ways to please her.

What happened next should have been predictable. When Shirley saw that I was anxious about losing her, she began to get bored with me. Gone was the challenge that had attracted her two years before. Instead, I had become just another guy pounding on her door and asking for favours. Our relationship was on the rocks.

One day after a particularly uninspiring date, I sat down

at a desk and spent two solid hours thinking about what was happening. This girl had been wrapped around my little finger two years ago, and now she was rapidly slipping away from me. What had gone wrong?

Suddenly, I realised the mistake I was making. I was treating myself with disrespect, grovelling and hoping for a handout. I grabbed a pen and wrote ten changes I was going to make in our relationship.

First, I decided to demonstrate self-respect and dignity, even if I lost the girl I now loved so deeply. Second, I determined to convey this attitude every time I got the chance: 'I am going somewhere in life, and I'm anxious to get there. I love you and hope you choose to go with me. If you do, I'll devote myself to you and try to make you happy. However, if you decide not to make the journey with me, then I'll find someone else. The decision is yours, and I'll accept it.' There were other elements to my plan, but they all centred on self-confidence and independence.

THE 'NEW APPROACH' WORKED

The first night that I applied the new approach was one of the most exhilarating experiences of my life. The girl who is now my wife saw me starting to slip away, and she reacted with alarm. We were riding in my car without talking. Shirley asked me to pull over to the curb and stop. When I did she put her arms around my neck and said, 'I'm afraid I'm losing you, and I don't know why. Do you still love me?' I noticed by the reflected light of the moon that she had tears in her eyes.

We crave what we can't attain, but we disrespect what we can't escape.

She obviously didn't hear my thumping heart as I made a little speech about my solitary journey in life. Our relationship was sealed that night, and we were married shortly thereafter. You see, I had re-established the challenge for Shirley, and she responded predictably.

The psychological force that produced our see-saw relationship is an important one, since it is almost universal in human nature. Forgive the redundancy, but I must restate the principle: We crave what we can't attain, but we disrespect what we can't escape. This axiom is particularly relevant in romantic matters and will probably influence your love life, too.

Let me cite another illustration that will put some meat on these bones. It is provided for us by Jack London, a classic American novelist who wrote adventure stories about life in the Yukon. The best known of his many short stories was entitled *To Build a Fire*, which was an incredible story about a man who was caught in a terrible blizzard. The temperature dropped to seventy degrees below zero and the man realised he was freezing to death. He tried to stave off the inevitable by killing his dog and warming his hands in the entrails. But the dog sensed danger and stayed out of reach.

The only remaining hope was to ignite some snow-covered branches and leaves scattered under a tree. The man had three matches in his parka, but would they be enough? The howling wind and icy vegetation would make it difficult to start a fire.

The first two matches flickered and went out. The man could not afford another failure. He put his back to the wind, cupped his trembling hands and struck the final match. Slowly, a little fire began to burn. He protected the flame with great intensity and began adding more leaves. His heart pounded wildly. He was making it! A life-giving fire would soon give him warmth. He was going to live!

Then suddenly, the wind blew some snow off a branch above the man's head. It fell directly on his tiny fire and snuffed it out. His last chance for survival ended with a sizzle. In despair, the man lay back on the snow and quietly froze to death.[1]

If you haven't read this dramatic story by Jack London, I hope you'll get a chance to do so. It not only pulls the reader into the desperation of the character, but it also makes a point relevant to our purposes. Romantic love is like that little flame. It is very tenuous in the beginning. Even though it has the potential of becoming a roaring fire, it must be protected and shielded from the wind. Those who become too aggressive and too desperate might as well be throwing snow on the sparks that remain. It is the quickest way to destroy what could have been a beautiful relationship.

FIRST OF ALL, RESPECT

Something changes the moment one of the two romantic partners begins to fear that the other may be slipping away. He complains about who she was with last night and whines about not being given enough attention. He parks his car near her house at night and spies on who's coming and going. He blows his top frequently and makes impossible demands. These signs of desperation quickly snuff out a romantic spark before it can grow into a flame of love. The key issue to understand here is the importance of respect in romantic affairs. It is the fuel that feeds the fire.

The key issue to understand here is the importance of respect in romantic affairs.

I heard of a young man who overlooked that simple principle. He was determined to win the affection of a girl who refused to even see him. He decided that the way to her heart was through the mail, so he began writing her a love letter every day. When she did not respond, he increased his output to three notes every twenty-four hours. In all, he wrote her more than seven hundred letters—and she married the postman.

Romantic love is one of those rare human endeavours that succeeds best when it requires the least effort. Those who pursue it the hardest are the most likely to fail. And speaking of people who try harder, no one beats a guy named Keith Ruff, whose love affair became the subject of an article in the *Los Angeles Times*. The headline read, 'Man Spends $20,000 Trying to Win Hand of Girl Who Can Say No'. This is the story:

A love-struck man holed-up in $200-a-day Washington hotel has spent, at latest estimate, close to $20,000 demonstrating to his beloved that he won't take 'no' for an answer to his marriage proposal.

On bended knee on Christmas Day, thirty-five-year-old Keith Ruff, once a stockbroker in Beverly Hills, proposed marriage to twenty-year-old Karine Bolstein, a cocktail waitress at a Washington restaurant. He met her in a shoe store last summer. The pair had gone out a few times over a two-month period before the proposal.

To his proposal, she looked down and said, 'no.'

Since then, Ruff has remained in Washington and demonstrated his wish that she reconsider by sending her everything but a partridge in a pear tree. That may be next.

He is, he thinks, 'close to spending all of my money. I'm not an Arab sheik.' The tokens of his affection include:

A Lear jet, placed on standby at the airport, 'in case she wanted to ride around'.

Between 3,000 and 5,000 flowers.

A limousine equipped with a bar and television, parked outside her door.

A gold ring.

$200 worth of champagne.

Catered lobster dinners.

Musicians to serenade her.

A clown to amuse her younger brother.

A man dressed as Prince Charming, bearing a glass slipper.

Biscuits, chocolates and perfume.

Sandwich-board wearers walking around her home and the restaurant where Bolstein works, conveying the message 'Mr. Dennis Keith Ruff **Loves** Ms Karine Bolstein'.

Balloons, which she promptly popped. 'What else would she do?' said the undaunted Ruff. 'The house was so full of flowers there was no room to walk around.'

For her father, a basket of nuts and $300 worth of cigars 'to pass out to his friends at the Labour Department. It may sound goofy, but I like him.'

For her mother, flowers at the French Embassy, where she works. 'I don't think her mother likes me. She called the police,' Ruff said. 'But I'll keep sending gifts to her also. How could anyone be so mad?'

For both her parents, a stepladder, 'so they might look at the relationship from a different angle.'

Unsurprisingly, Ruff said he has 'a very, very strange monetary situation.' He has not worked in some time, describing himself as being of independent means. 'I don't care how many job offers I get. I'm not interested in any of them,' Ruff said. 'I'd rather think about her than sit at a job.' He said he will spend his last dime and will beg for money if he has to, that he will keep on trying for ten years, twenty years. I'll ask her to marry me 50,000 times.

It doesn't matter how many times she says no. I will do everything in my power that's not absurd or against any reasonable law. I wouldn't stop if she became a nun. I've never felt this way before!

Bolstein, meanwhile, said she is flattered, but too young to get married. She also said the house looks like a funeral parlour.

Ruff said, 'I don't want to force her to love me, but I can't stop. Maybe this makes her nervous, but at least she gets to smile along with being nervous. Anybody would like it somewhat.'

Ruff said many people he talks to are sceptical. 'People

would say my love is strange,' he said, 'but our whole society is falling apart because of the way people love. What is dating? Some guy putting his paws all over you?

'My friends in LA know how many women I've gone out with. I didn't like being a womaniser. I believe in the old values. I found the woman I love.' Ruff said he spends a lot of time in his hotel room planning what to do next and occasionally crying. Bolstein, meanwhile, has been asked for her autograph where she works and has had a drink there named after her, a concoction of gin, vodka and rum entitled, 'She Won't'.

Ruff said Bolstein called him once. 'But I hung up on her. I didn't like what she said. Reality, to me is disturbing,' Ruff said. 'I'd rather close my eyes and see her face.

'Fantasy is where I'm living. I'm living with hope.

'And some very big bills.' [2]

There are several things ol' Ruff needs to know about women, assuming Miss Bolstein hasn't got the message across to him by now. He could cry in his hotel room for the next fifty years without generating the tiniest bit of sympathy from her. And that jet airplane doesn't mean a hill of beans to her either. Very few women are attracted to snivelling men who crawl, who bribe, who whine and make fools of themselves in view of the whole world. Tell me, who wants to marry an unambitious 'weirdo' who grovels in the dirt like a whipped puppy? Good-bye, romance! Hello, poorhouse.

On a much smaller scale, of course, the same mistake is made by 'singles' in other places. They reveal their hopes and dreams too early in the game and scare the socks off potential lovers. Divorcees fall into the same trap—especially women who need a man to support them and their children. Male candidates for that assignment are rarities and are sometimes recruited

Romantic love is one of those rare human endeavours that succeeds best when it requires the least effort.

like All-American athletes. I've seen no better illustration than the following item, also appearing in the *Los Angeles Times*.

Q. I am a recently divorced, professional man with an unusual problem. I hope you can help me. A woman I dated once called me before I even had a chance to make a second date with her and wanted to know why I hadn't called her again. After our second date she began to call almost daily with offers for dinner, something funny she'd read and thought I'd enjoy, etc. The crazy part is that this same routine has started with another woman I'm just beginning to ask out. If such behaviour is typical, maybe I should have stayed married! How do I extricate myself from this frenzied dating and have a nice, quiet social life? [3]

Isn't it obvious what is occurring here? The women being dated by this 'professional man' are chasing him like a hound after a rabbit. And predictably, his natural impulse is to run. If they are interested in pulling him towards them, they simply must not invade his territory. Instead, they should maintain a sense of decorum and let the chips fall where they may.

Let me illustrate graphically what is occurring in situations of this nature. It involves a simple demonstration with the hands with which we can represent Partner A and Partner B. I call it 'the tender trap'.

PARTNER A  PARTNER B

Partners A and B decide to get married and live happily

ever after. At some point along the way, however, Partner B begins to feel trapped in the relationship. Their spouse offends or bores them in numerous ways, and they resent those five constraining words ' 'til death do us part'.

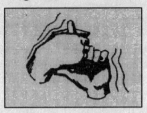

PARTNER A   PARTNER B

In order to deal with this sense of containment—this restriction of freedom—Partner B moves gradually to the right, away from Partner A.

PARTNER A   PARTNER B

Partner A observes Partner B's retreat and reacts with alarm. Their impulse is to pursue Partner B, closing the gap even tighter than before.

PARTNER A   PARTNER B

Partner B makes a more obvious attempt to flee, but in a moment of desperation, Partner A jumps on Partner B and clutches them with all their strength. Partner B struggles to escape and will surely run the moment they gain release.

PARTNER A

Partner A then droops in loneliness, wondering how something so beautiful became so sour.

Instead . . .

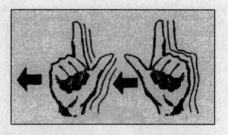

PARTNER A   PARTNER B

Regardless of what commonsense tells us to the contrary, Partner A's best chance of attracting and holding a suffocating lover is to pull backwards slightly, conveying freedom for Partner B and respect for themselves in the process. Curiously, Partner B often moves towards Partner A when this occurs. We've all observed this need for 'space' in human relationships, but the concept is still difficult to comprehend when it pertains to ourselves and our loved ones.

TIPS TO HELP YOU 'LOVE TOUGH'

Well, I think the point has been made. Let me get very specific with those of you who are single but wish someday to marry. (No insult is intended to those who are single by design and wish to remain unmarried. That is a legitimate choice that should be respected by friends and family, alike.) Listed below are seventeen suggestions that will help you conform to the principles of 'loving toughness' in matters of the heart.

Who wants to marry an unambitious weirdo who grovels in the dirt like a whipped puppy?

1. Don't let the relationship move too fast in its infancy. The phrase 'too hot not to cool down' has validity. Relationships that begin in a frenzy frequently burn themselves out. Take it one step at a time.

2. Don't discuss your personal inadequacies and flaws in great detail when the relationship is new. No matter how warm and accepting your friend may be, any great reveltion of low self-esteem or embarrassing weaknesses can be fatal when interpersonal 'valleys' occur. And they will occur.

3. Remember that respect precedes love. Build it stone upon stone.

4. Don't call too often on the phone or give the other person an opportunity to get tired of you.

5. Don't be too quick to reveal your desire to get married— or that you think you've just found Mr Wonderful or Miss Marvelous. If your partner has not arrived at the same conclusion, you'll throw them into a panic.

6. Most important: Relationships are constantly being

'tested' by cautious lovers who like to nibble at the bait before swallowing the hook. This testing procedure takes many forms, but it usually involves pulling backwards from the other person to see what will happen. Perhaps a foolish fight is initiated. Maybe two weeks will pass without a phone call. Or sometimes flirtation occurs with a rival. In each instance, the question being asked is 'How important am I to you, and what would you do if you lost me?' An even more basic issue lies below that one. It wants to know, 'How free am I to leave if I want to?' It is incredibly important in these instances to appear poised, secure, and equally independent. Do not grasp the other person and beg for mercy. Some people remain single throughout their life because they cannot resist the temptation to grovel when the test occurs.

7. Extending the same concept, keep in mind that virtually every dating relationship that continues for a year or more and seems to be moving towards marriage will be given the ultimate test. A break-up will occur, motivated by only one of the lovers. The rejected individual should know that their future together depends on the skill with which they handle the crisis. If the hurting individual can remain calm, as Shirley did with me, the next two steps may be reconciliation and marriage. It often happens that way. If not, then no amount of pleading will change anything.

8. Do not depend entirely upon one another for the satisfaction of every emotional need. Maintain interests and activities outside that romantic relationship, even after marriage.

9. Guard against selfishness in your love affair. Neither should do all the giving. I once broke up with a girl

because she let me take her to nice places, bring her flowers, buy her lunch, etc. I wanted to do these things but expected her to reciprocate in some way. She didn't.

10. Beware of blindness to obvious warning signs that tell you that your potential husband or wife is basically disloyal, hateful, spiritually uncommitted, hooked on drugs or alcohol, given to selfishness, etc. Believe me, a bad marriage is far worse than the most lonely instance of being single.

11. In the early part of the dating relationship, treat the other person with respect and expect the same in return. A man should open doors for a woman on a formal evening; a woman should speak respectfully of her escort when in public, etc. If you don't preserve this respectful attitude when the foundations of marriage are being laid, it will be virtually impossible to construct them later.

12. Do not equate human worth with flawless beauty or handsomeness! If you require physical perfection in your mate, they may make the same demands of you. Don't let love escape you because of the false values of your culture.

13. If genuine love has escaped you thus far, don't begin believing 'no one would ever want me'. That is a deadly trap that can destroy you emotionally! Millions of people are looking for someone to love. The problem is finding one another!

14. Regardless of how brilliant the love affair has been, take time to 'check your assumptions' with your partner before committing yourself to marriage. It is surprising how often men and women

Extreme dependency can be . . . deadly to a love affair.

plunge towards matrimony without ever becoming aware of major differences in expectation between them. For example:

a. Do you want to have children? How soon? How many?
b. Where will you live?
c. Will your wife work? How soon? How about after children are born?
d. Who will lead in the relationship? What does that really mean?
e. How will you relate to your in-laws?
f. How will money be spent?
g. How important will spiritual matters be in the marriage?

These and dozens of other 'assumptions' should be discussed item by item with the help of a premarital counsellor. Many future struggles can be avoided by coming to terms with potential areas of disagreement. If the differences are great enough, it is even possible that the marriage should never occur.

15. Sexual familiarity can be deadly to a relationship. In addition to the many moral, spiritual, and physical reasons for remaining virgins until marriage, there are numerous psychological and interpersonal advantages as well. Though it's an old-fashioned notion, perhaps, it is still true that men do not respect 'easy' women and often become bored with those who have held nothing in reserve. Likewise, women often disrespect men who have only one thing on their minds. Both sexes need to remember how to use a very ancient word. It's pronounced 'No!'

16. Country singer Tom T. Hall wrote a song in which he revealed an understanding of the concept we have been describing. His lyric read, 'If you hold love too loosely then it flies away; if you hold love too tightly, it'll die. It's one of the mysteries of life'.[4] Hall's observation is accurate. If the commitment between a man and a woman is given insufficient importance in their lives, it will wither like a plant without water. The whole world knows that much. But fewer lovers seem to realise that extreme dependency can be just as deadly to a love affair. It has been said that the person who needs the other least will normally be in control of the relationship. I believe that to be true.

17. There is nothing about marriage that eliminates the basic need for freedom and respect in romantic interactions. Keep the mystery and the dignity in your relationship. If the other partner begins to feel trapped and withdraws for a time, grant them some space and pull back yourself. Do not build a cage around that person. Instead, release your grip with confidence while never appeasing immorality or destructive behaviour. For more information on this topic, read *Love Must Be Tough*.

These suggestions are not guaranteed to win the hand of a lover, of course, but they will certainly beat the approach of Mr Keith Ruff. And you'll save $20,000 in the process!

8

QUESTIONS FROM THE EDGE

CHAPTER EIGHT

I want to make sure I understand the concept of 'Love Must Be Tough'. If you had to reduce the idea to its lowest common denominator, what would it be?

The bottom line is showing respect for yourself and for another person, which is the foundation on which romantic love is built. It is refusing to beg, plead, and whine if a partner does not feel about you the way you feel about them. To build a cage around someone in order to hold that person against their will just makes the 'caged' one more desperate to escape.

The idea that Love Must Be Tough dictates that we will be willing to set another person free—even if it causes us great pain to let go. When we do this, we maximise the chances that that loved one will not leave, because the cage door has been opened and self-respect has been affirmed.

2. You said the concept has applications other than this narrow definition. Talk about that in the context of marriage.

As I indicated, Love Must Be Tough applies wherever two or more personalities interact. Let me illustrate. One of the secrets to my beautiful marriage to Shirley, which has now lasted for thirty-four years, is that we have been careful to defend what we call 'the line of respect' between us.

For example, suppose I work in my office two hours longer than usual on a particular night, knowing Shirley is preparing a special candlelight dinner. The phone sits there on my desk, but I'm too selfish to make a brief call to explain. As the evening wears on, Shirley wraps the cold food in foil and puts it in the refrigerator.

Then suppose when I finally get home, I do not apologise. Instead, I sit down with a newspaper and abruptly tell Shirley to get my dinner ready. You can bet there'll be a few minutes of fireworks in the Dobson household! Shirley will rightfully interpret my behaviour as insulting and will move to defend the 'line of respect' between us. Then we will talk it out, and next time I'll be more considerate.

Now suppose Shirley knows I need the car at 2.00 p.m. for some important purpose, but she deliberately keeps me waiting. Perhaps she is in a restaurant with a lady friend, drinking coffee and talking. Meanwhile, I'm pacing the floor at home wondering where she is. It is very likely that my wife will hear about my dissatisfaction when she gets home. The 'line of respect' has been violated, and we will work to re-establish it.

What is at stake in these examples, both of which are petty, is a foundation of mutual accountability. In order to live with someone for a lifetime, two people have to establish some ground rules that will help them maintain harmony and order. Mutual respect is the centrepiece of that understanding between them. When their rules are violated, a mild confrontation is in order.

What I'm saying is that minor conflict plays a positive role in maintaining the health of a relationship, provided it doesn't generate too much anger. In families where one partner permits the other to behave in hurtful and disrespectful ways, the unhealthy behaviour is not checked and corrected. It tends to get worse with the passage of time. In extreme cases, a wife may even choose to ignore her husband's sexual unfaithfulness for fear he will leave her if she objects. Thus, she reveals disrespect for herself and tempts her husband to do even more outrageous things. Her anger is stored instead of ventilated and will eventually erupt like a volcano. Divorces are made of such things.

Learning how to fight properly and deciding what to fight about is one of the secrets to a successful marriage. It usually comes down to the 'line of respect' one way or the other.

3. How does a woman know when she is grovelling and treating herself disrespectfully? I'm not sure if I'm being used as a doormat or not.

Just ask yourself if you feel good about the relationship. Are you making all the phone calls to the other person? Do they tell you the truth invariably? Have you been 'stood up' without a reasonable excuse? Do you fear they are slipping away, and is that causing you to 'grab and hold'? Are you tolerating insults thatothers would not accept? Do they show evidence of 'cherishing' you and wanting to make you happy? Do they tell your secrets and make comments about you in public that embarrass you? Are they physically abusive at times? Do they ever 'reach' for you instead of you reaching for them? Do your friends ever say, 'Why do you put up with all this stuff?'

Minor conflict plays a positive role in maintaining the health of a relationship.

These are questions that only you can answer. But if

you are honest with yourself, you will have no difficulty identifying disrespectful components to your relationship. If you come up with the wrong answers, the solution is not to beg your partner to do better. It is to pull back and see if they follow. If not, you're better off looking for someone else.

4. You said earlier that guys should open doors for girls, offer them their seats on buses—that kind of thing. Would you elaborate on that suggestion? That seems kind of out of date today.

It is unfortunate that these expressions of courtesy have become less fashionable in our culture. The issue here is a matter of respect between the sexes, which makes everything work better. Girls and women should insist that they are treated with dignity, especially when they're out on a date or in more formal situations.

But it works both ways. There are many opportunities for a girl to show respect to a man, too. She can serve him coffee or iron his shirt or style her hair in a way he likes. She can find subtle ways to make him feel good about himself. As someone said, a man usually falls in love with a woman who asks questions he can answer brilliantly.

> *A man usually falls in love with a woman who asks questions he can answer brilliantly.*

For some reason, people who are into political correctness become very angry over this issue of how the sexes relate to each other. They would have them compete with each other in an atmosphere of one-upmanship. They believe men and women are identical except for obvious reproductive differences. It is not true.

We are unique in countless ways. And we relate best to each other when we show deference and honour to the opposite sex in our casual interactions. This issue of respect is foundational to all human relationships. When a couple doesn't take time to show it, they are on shaky ground.

5. My boyfriend and I are always fighting and arguing. We just can't seem to get along for more than a few days, even though I think we love each other. Would we probably learn to be more compatible if we decide to get married?

I think it would be very risky to press ahead with marriage in view of the warning signs you're seeing. At the very least, you should seek premarital counselling from someone who is skilled in providing this service. There are some excellent tests available that indicate probable incompatibility and trouble spots. Not only will these tests help you make the right decision about marriage, but they can teach you how to relate better to each other if you do choose to stay together.

We relate to each other when we show deference and honour.

By the way, the following diagram may also be of some help to you. Locate the words that characterise how the two of you get along, and then decide whether you have a healthy or an unhealthy relationship.

6. The note your dad wrote to your mum before they were married was touching, but I don't think it was realistic. He promised to stay with her no matter what! That was very risky. We can't foresee the future, and I don't think it's wise to say what a person will do at a critical moment.

I disagree strongly. When you consider the many pressures that couples face today, only an iron-clad determination will hold them together for a lifetime. Those who go into marriage with a mushy commitment are likely to

LIGHT RELATIONSHIP

LIGHTHEARTED   FUN

FREE   UNPOSSESSIVE

SEXUALLY RESERVED   MYSTERIOUS

MANY 'OTHER' INTERESTS & PEOPLE

EASY COME, EASY GO

MIDDLE GROUND BETWEEN THE EXTREMES

'OWNERSHIP' OF PARTNER

MANY DEMANDS

ANGER AT FAILURE OF PARTNER TO DELIVER

POSSESSIVE   SEXUALLY PERMISSIVE

NO MYSTERY   UNHAPPY

LACK OF OTHER INTERESTS & PEOPLE

HEAVY RELATIONSHIP

EXCELLENT

AVERAGE

POOR

HEALTH OF RELATIONSHIP

TEARS—CONFLICT

wobble and fall apart when the hard times come. And as we all know, hard times will come.

I'm reminded of my friends, Keith and Mary Korstjens, who have been married more than forty years. Shortly after their honeymoon, Mary was stricken with polio and became a quadriplegic. The doctors informed her that she would be confined to a wheelchair for the rest of her life.

Nevertheless, Keith never wavered in his commitment to Mary. For all these years, he has bathed and dressed her, carried her to and from her bed, taken her to the bathroom, brushed her teeth, and combed her hair. Keith could have divorced Mary in 1957 and looked for a new, healthier wife. But he never even considered it. I admire Keith not only for 'hanging tough', but for continuing to love and cherish his wife. This couple has been an inspiration to thousands over the past four decades.[1]

Without the kind of commitment my dad made to my mum, their marriage would never have survived.

7. Is it possible to love someone and not feel it?

It certainly is—because love is more than a feeling. It is primarily a decision. Married couples who misunderstand this point will have serious problems when the feeling of love disappears for a time. As we'll discuss later, couples who genuinely love each other will experience times of closeness, times when they feel apathetic, and times when they are irritated and moody. That's just the way emotions operate. What, then, will hold them steady as feelings bounce all over the landscape? The source of constancy is a commitment of the will. You simply make up your mind not to be blown off track by fluctuating and unreliable emotions.

8. Do you believe in love at first sight?

No way, José! Love at first sight is a physical and emotional impossibility. Why? Because, as I've indicated, love is much more than a romantic feeling. It is more than a sexual attraction or the thrill of the chase or a desire to marry someone. These are responses that can occur 'at first sight', and they might even lead to the genuine thing in time. But these feelings are usually very temporary, and they do not mean the person who experiences them is 'in love'. I wish everyone understood that fact!

Genuine love . . . is an expression of the deepest appreciation for another human being.

The primary difference between romantic excitement and real love is where the emphasis lies. Infatuation tends to be very selfish in nature. A person may say, 'I can't believe what is happening to me. This is the most fantastic thing I've ever experienced! I must be in love.' Notice that they're not talking about the other person. They're excited about their own gratification. Such an individual hasn't fallen in love with someone else; they have fallen in love with love!

Genuine love, by contrast, is an expression of the deepest appreciation for another human being. It is an awareness of their needs, and strengths, and character. It shares the longings, hopes, and dreams of that other person. It is unselfish, giving and caring. And believe me, these are not attitudes someone just 'falls into', like tumbling into a ditch.

I have developed this kind of lifelong love for my wife, but it wasn't something I fell into. I grew into it through the years. I had to know her thoroughly before I could appreciate the depth of her character and the nuances of her personality, which I now cherish. The familiarity from which love has grown simply could not have occurred on 'some enchanted evening, across a crowded room'.

Again, you can't 'fall in love' with an unknown object, regardless of how pretty, handsome, or sexy it is.

9. You said you've been happily married for more than thirty years now. Have you ever been tempted to be unfaithful to your wife? What are the danger points that we should watch for?

Honestly, I have never even considered cheating on Shirley. The very thought of hurting her and inviting God's wrath are more than enough to keep me on the straight and narrow. Furthermore, I would never destroy the specialness we shared for all these years. But even in marriages that are based on this kind of commitment, Satan will try to undermine them.

He laid a trap for me during a time of particular vulnerability. Shirley and I had been married for just a few years when we had a minor fuss. It was no big deal but we both were pretty agitated at the time. I got in the car and drove around for about an hour to cool off. Then when I was on the way home, a very attractive girl drove up beside me in her car and smiled. She was obviously flirting with me. Then she slowed down, looked back, and turned into a side street. I knew she was inviting me to follow her.

I didn't take the bait. I just went on home and made up with Shirley. But I thought later about how vicious Satan had been to take advantage of the momentary conflict between us. The Scripture refers to the devil as 'a roaring lion . . . seeking whom he might devour' (1 Peter. 5:8 KJV). I can see how true that description really is. He knew his best opportunity to damage our marriage was during that hour or two when we were irritated with each other. That is typical of his strategy. He'll lay a trap for you, too, and it'll probably come at a time of vulnerability. Beautiful, enticing, forbidden fruit will be offered to you when your 'hunger' is greatest. If you are foolish enough to reach for it, your fingers will sink into the rotten mush. That's the way sin operates in our lives. It promises everything. It delivers nothing but disgust and heartache.

Someone said it this way: 'All you need to grow the finest crop of weeds is a tiny crack in your pavement.'

10. I have a great fear that I will someday be divorced. I've been through it with my parents and watched several of my uncles and aunts. It is very hard on everybody. I'd rather not get married than to run that risk. Is it possible to protect yourself from a divorce today?

You're not the only member of your generation who worries about the odds against successful marriages. That concern showed up in a popular song sung a few years ago by Carly Simon. The lyrics are devastating. They say, in effect, 'It is impossible to achieve intimacy in marriage, and our life together will be lonely, meaningless, and sterile. But if that's what you want . . . we'll marry'. Read them for yourself:

> My father sits at night with no lights on:
> His cigarette glows in the dark.
> The living room is still
> I walk by, no remark.
> I tiptoe past the master bedroom where
> My mother reads her magazines.
> I hear her call sweet dreams.
> But I forget how to dream.
>
> But you say it's time we moved in together
> And raise a family of our own, you and me.
> Well, that's the way I've always heard it should be:
> You want to marry, we'll marry.

My friends from college they're all married now.
They have their houses and their lawns.
They have their silent noons.
Tearful nights, angry dawns.
Their children hate them for the things they're not:
They hate themselves for what they are.
And yet they drink, they laugh.
Close the wound, hide the scar.

But you say it's time we moved in together
And raise a family of our own, you and me.
Well, that's the way I've always heard it should be:
You want to marry, we'll marry.

You say that we can keep our love alive;
Babe, all I know is what I see.
The couples cling and claw
And drown in love's debris.
You say we'll soar like two birds through the clouds,
But soon you'll cage me on your shelf.
I'll never learn to be just me first by myself.

Well, OK, it's time we moved in together
And raise a family of our own, you and me.
Well, that's the way I've always heard it should be:
You want to marry me, we'll marry.
We'll marry.[2]

While I understand the pessimism expressed in this song, I disagree emphatically with its message. The family was God's idea, not our own, and it is still a wonderful institution.

Furthermore, it is a myth that marriages are destined to fail. Sixty-one per cent of people living in the United States are married, twelve-three per cent have never been married, eight per cent are widowed, and only eight per cent are divorced. Seventy-five per cent of families with children are headed by two married parents.[3] Despite what you hear about disintegrating families, most of us live within them and are happy about this fact.

We do have to acknowledge, however, that marriages are

The family was God's idea, not our own, and it is still a wonderful institution.

fragile. They must be nurtured and protected if they are to survive for a lifetime. If ignored, they will wither like plants without water. The natural tendency of everything in the universe is to move from order to disorder. If you buy a new car today, it will steadily deteriorate from the day you drive it home. Your body starts to die the day you are born. A house has to be repainted every few years. If you put a brick on an empty building plot and leave it there long enough, it will turn to dust. Even the sun is slowly burning itself out.

Nothing in the physical world moves from disorder to order without intelligence and energy being applied to it. This is what is wrong with the theory of evolution, which is the only belief system asserting that things move upwards towards perfection on their own and without the benefit of intelligent design. It contradicts everything we can observe and examine.

The Scriptures describe this downward tug on the universe and its inhabitants. King David said it like this:

> In the beginning you laid the
>   foundations of the earth,
>   and the heavens are the work of your hands.
> They will perish, but you remain;
>   they will all wear out like a garment.
> Like clothing you will change them
>   and they will be discarded.

But you remain the same,
  and your years will never end
(Psalm 102:25–27).

Other scriptures speak of a curse that is on the earth and
its inhabitants. We might call it 'the law of disintegration'.
Theologians refer to the curse as the
consequences of sin and trace its origin
to the disobedience of Adam and Eve in

Marriages are fragile.

the Garden of Eden. God had warned Adam that he would
'surely die' if he ate of the tree of knowledge of good and
evil. After Adam yielded to temptation, the Creator pronounced this death sentence on him:

Cursed is the ground because of you;
  through painful toil you will eat of it
  all the days of your life.
It will produce thorns and thistles for you,
  and you will eat the plants of the field.
By the sweat of your brow
  you will eat your food
until you return to the ground,
  since from it you were taken;
for dust you are
  and to dust you will return
(Genesis. 3:17–19).

My point is that this 'law of disintegration' also relates to
marriage. Human relationships are governed by the same
principle. The natural tendency is for people to drift away
from each other. That is exactly what happens when husbands and wives become too busy or distracted to maintain
their love. If they don't take the time for romantic activities
and experiences that draw them together, something precious begins to slip away. It doesn't have to be that way, of

course, but the downward pull will do its damage if efforts are not made to counteract the force.

12. What, then, can a person do to keep a marriage from drifting?

Husbands and wives need to return regularly to the kind of romantic activities that drew them together in the first place. They need to put some fun and laughter into their lives, which otherwise can get dreary and oppressive.

A few years ago, Shirley and I found ourselves in that kind of situation where we had almost forgotten how to play. We finally became fed up and decided to do something about it. We loaded the car and headed for a winter wonderland in Mammoth, California. There we spent the weekend skiing and eating and laughing together. That night we built a fire in the hearth and talked for hours while our favourite music played on the stereo. We felt like we were kids again.

To keep a marriage vibrant and healthy, you simply have to give it some attention. Water the plant, give it sunlight, and it will grow. Put it in a dark, dry corner, and it is likely to die.

13. My boyfriend doesn't talk to me very much. He's just a very quiet and shy person. Will he always be this way? I just wish he'd tell me what he's thinking and feeling.

Your question reminds me of the twelve-year-old boy who had never spoken a word. His parents and siblings thought he couldn't talk because they'd never heard his voice. Then one day the boy's mother placed some soup in front of him and he ate a spoonful. Then he pushed the bowl away and said, 'This is slop, and I won't eat any more of it!'

The family was ecstatic. He'd actually spoken a complete sentence. They all jumped around gleefully, and his father said, 'Why haven't you ever talked to us before?'

The boy replied, 'Because, up until now everything has been OK.'

Maybe your boyfriend will also surprise you someday with a flurry of words, but I doubt it. Shyness results from an inborn temperament that tends to be very persistent throughout life. Research shows that approximately fifteen per cent of children are genetically programmed to be somewhat introvert like your friend and that most of them will always be that way.[4] It appears that some people just seem to be born 'noisy', and others prefer to keep their thoughts to themselves. Your boyfriend may be one of the latter.

> *Husbands and wives need to return regularly to the kind of romantic activities that drew them together in the first place.*

If you choose to marry him, I hope you'll do so with your eyes wide open. You're probably not going to change him. Many women fall in love with the strong, silent type and then they resent their men for the rest of their lives because they won't talk to them.

You should also know that men are naturally less verbal than women. They typically find it tougher to share their feelings and express their ideas. A particular man may have about 25,000 words to say per day and his wife has 50,000. Thus, he comes home with his quota spent, and she still has 37,000 to go. It is a very common source of frustration among women. But that's the way it is.

14. I'm the boyfriend who doesn't talk very much. I've been that way all my life. Part of the problem is that I just don't like to reveal what I'm feeling. But also, I don't know how to talk to people. I get really uncomfortable when I'm

with people and I'm expected to say something. Can you give me some hints about how to express myself?

It might help you to understand the basics of good conversation. Let me ask you to imagine that the two of us are facing each other about eight feet apart. You have four tennis balls in your hands, and you toss one of them to me. Instead of throwing the ball back, however, I hold it and wait for you to toss another to me. Eventually all four balls are in my hands. We stand there looking at each other awkwardly and wondering what to do next. The game is over.

Good conversation is something like that game of catch. One person throws an idea or a comment to the other, and they toss it back. But if that second person doesn't return it, the game ends. Both players feel awkward and wish they could be somewhere else. Let me illustrate further.

Suppose I say to my son when he comes home in the afternoon, 'How did it go in school today?' If he answers, 'Fine,' he has caught the ball and held it. We have nothing more to say to each other unless I can come up with another comment—another 'ball' to throw to him.

But if my son says, 'I had a good day because I got an A in my history test,' he has caught the ball and thrown it back. I can then ask, 'Was it a difficult test?' or, 'Did you study hard for it?' or 'I'll bet you're proud of yourself.'

If my son only replies, 'Yes,' he has wrecked the game again. To keep the conversation going, he needs to throw back something of substance, such as, 'It was a tough examination, but it was fair.' Then our 'game' can be continued.

I hope you see that the art of talking to people is really very simple. It's just a matter of throwing the conversational ball back and forth. Unfortunately, kids and teenagers are notorious for holding what has been tossed to them—especially when responding to adults. They resort to nine words (and word phrases) that are conversation killers: 'I dunno', 'Maybe', 'I forget', 'Huh?' 'Nope', 'Yeah', 'I guess so', 'Who—me?' and 'He did it.' End of discussion.

As for your relationship with a future wife, it won't be enough to just throw the ball back to her. She's going to want you to be more intimate than that. She'll need to know how you feel about her, what you dream about, things that upset you, what you'd like her to do, how you feel about God, etc. You can learn to put these thoughts into words, even though you will probably never be a big talker. I suggest that you push yourself in this direction rather than saying, 'That's just how I am'. Your wife will probably have to make some changes to accommodate you, too.

That's what a good marriage is all about.

9

GETTING ALONG
WITH YOUR
PARENTS

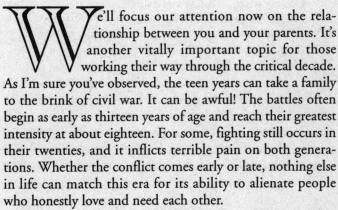

We'll focus our attention now on the relationship between you and your parents. It's another vitally important topic for those working their way through the critical decade. As I'm sure you've observed, the teen years can take a family to the brink of civil war. It can be awful! The battles often begin as early as thirteen years of age and reach their greatest intensity at about eighteen. For some, fighting still occurs in their twenties, and it inflicts terrible pain on both generations. Whether the conflict comes early or late, nothing else in life can match this era for its ability to alienate people who honestly love and need each other.

At least, that's the way family life often plays out today. I'm sure there has always been friction between parents and children, but the nature of it has changed radically. The culture that once was supportive and respectful of parents has now become the worst enemy of the family. Let me illustrate.

The artistic creations produced by a society at a given time don't spring from a vacuum. They reflect the opinions and beliefs commonly held by its people. That being true, we can measure change in attitudes by looking at the evolution of music that has occurred in recent years. Let's go back to 1953 when the most popular song in the United States was sung by Eddie Fisher, and was titled *Oh, My Papa*. Here's a portion of the lyrics:

> Oh, my papa, to me he was so wonderful
> Oh, my papa, to me he was so good.
> No one could be so gentle and so lovable,
> Oh, my papa, he always understood.
> Gone are the days when he would take me on his knee
> And with a smile he'd change my tears to laughter.
>
> Oh, my papa, so funny and adorable,
> Always the clown, so funny in his way,
> Oh, my papa, to me he was so wonderful
> Deep in my heart I miss him so today,
> Oh, my papa. Oh, my papa.[1]

That sentimental song accurately reflected the way many people felt about their fathers at that time in our history. Oh sure, there were conflicts and disagreements, but family was family. When all was said and done, parents were entitled to respect and loyalty, and they usually received it from their children.

THAT WAS THEN . . . THIS IS NOW

By the time I had reached college age, things were starting to change. The subject of conflict between parents and teenagers began to appear as a common theme in artistic creations. The movie *Rebel without a Cause* featured a screen idol named James Dean who seethed with anger at his 'Old Man'. Marlon Brando starred in *The Wild One,* another film with rebellion as its theme. Rock-'n'-roll music portrayed it, too.

Some early rock-'n'-roll lyrics mixed rebellious messages

with humour, such as a number-one hit from 1958 called *Yakkety-Yak (Don't Talk Back)*. But what began as musical humour turned decidedly bitter in the late sixties. Everyone in those days was talking about the 'generation gap' that had erupted between young people and their parents. Teenagers and college students vowed they'd never again trust anyone over thirty, and their anger towards parents began to percolate. The Doors released a song in 1968 entitled *The End*, in which Jim Morrison fanaticised about killing his father. It concludes with gunshots followed by horrible grunts and groans.[3]

BUT WAIT! IT GETS WORSE!

In 1984, Twisted Sister released *We're Not Gonna Take It*, which referred to a father as a 'disgusting slob' who was 'worthless and weak'.[4] Then he was blasted out the window of a second-storey apartment. This theme of killing parents showed up regularly in the decade that followed. A group called Suicidal Tendencies released a recording in 1983 called, *I Saw Your Mummy*. Here is an excerpt of the gory lyrics:

> I saw your mummy and your mummy's dead.
> I watched her as she bled,
> Chewed-off toes on her chopped-off feet.
> I took a picture because I thought it was neat.
>
> I saw your mummy, and your mummy's dead.
> I saw her lying in a pool of red;
> I think it's the greatest thing I'll ever see—
> Your dead mummy lying in front of me.[5]

For sheer banality, nothing yet produced can match *Momma's Gotta Die Tonight*, by Ice-T and Body Count.[6]

The album sold 500,000 copies and featured its wretched lyrics on the CD jacket. Most of them are unfit to quote here, but they involved graphic descriptions of the rapper's mother being burned in her bed, then beaten to death with a baseball bat she had given him as a present, and finally the mutilation of the corpse into 'little bitty pieces'. What incredible violence! There was not a hint of guilt or remorse expressed by the rapper while telling us of this murder. In fact, he called his mother a 'racist b____h', and laughed while chanting, 'Burn, Mama, burn'. My point is that the most popular music of our culture went from the inspiration of *Oh, My Papa* to the horrors of *Mumma's Gotta Die Tonight* in scarcely more than a generation. And we have to wonder, where do we go from here?

BOMBARDED BY ANTI-FAMILY RHETORIC

One thing is certain: Your generation has been bombarded with more anti-family rhetoric than any that preceded it. When added to equally disturbing messages about drug usage, sex, and violence against women, the impact has to be considered formid-able. Remember that teenagers (and preteens) not only hear such lyrics once or twice. The words are burned into their minds. They are memorised, sung, and quoted. And the rock stars who perform them become idols to many impressionable teenagers.

Your generation has been bombarded with more anti-family rhetoric than any that preceded it.

MTV, which promotes the worst stuff available, is telecast into 231,000,000 households in seventy-five countries, more than any other cable programme.[7] Though it will not be popular for me to say it, I believe many of the problems that plague your generation can be traced to this venom pumped into its veins by the entertainment industry in general.

Although I never identified with those who hated their parents, there were times when I thought my folks were 'yakety-yaking' too much. I remember working with my father one day when I was fifteen years old. We were cutting the grass and cleaning-out the garage on a very hot day. For some reason, Dad was particularly cranky that afternoon. He moaned at me for everything I did, even when I hurried. Finally, he yelled at me for something petty, and that did it. I just threw down my rake.

Defiantly, I walked across our garden and down the street while my dad demanded that I come back. It was one of the few times I ever took him on like that! I meandered around town for a while, wondering what would happen when I finally went home. Then I strolled over to my cousin's house on the other side of town. That night, I admitted to his father that I'd had a bad fight with my dad and he didn't know where I was. My uncle persuaded me to call home and assure my parents that I was safe. With knees quaking, I phoned my dad.

'Stay there,' he said. 'I'm coming over.

To say that I was scared would be an understatement. In a short time Dad arrived and asked to see me alone.

'Bo,' he began, 'I didn't treat you right this afternoon. I was riding your back for no good reason, and I want you to know I'm sorry. Your mum and I want you to come on home now.'

He made a friend for life.

Not all family fights end so lovingly, of course. In fact, I'll bet you've been through some tough moments of your own. How about it? Have you had royal shootouts with your mum and dad? Do you harbour deep resentment for things they've said or done? Have you wounded them by your defiance and independence? Are there scars on your relationship that you wish weren't there? Why does it have to be that way?

Admittedly, some of those to whom I am writing have been abused by their parents and their anger is rooted in that pain. But let's assume you are not one of them. Your mother and father love you like crazy and would endure any sacrifice to give you what you need. Why, then, are there such strong negative feelings between you? Let's take a moment to examine the causes of family feuds and offer a few suggestions for improvement.

THERE IT IS AGAIN . . . POWER!

At the risk of revisiting issues we have already covered, the basic source of conflict between generations is that old bugbear—power. It is defined as control—control of others, control of our circumstances, and especially control of ourselves. The lust for it lies deep within the human spirit. We all want to be the boss, and that impulse begins very early in life. Studies show that one-day-old infants actually 'reach' for control of the adults around them. Even at this tender age, they behave in ways designed to get their guardians to meet their needs.

> *The basic source of conflict between generations is that old bugbear—power.*

The desire for power is apparent when a toddler runs from his mother in a supermarket or when a ten-year-old refuses to do their homework or when a husband and wife fight over money. We see it when an elderly woman refuses to move to a nursing home. The common thread between these examples is the passion to run our own lives—and everything else if given the chance. People vary in the intensity of this urge, but it seems to motivate all of us to one degree or another.

As implied in a previous chapter, the grab for control is

what produces most of the conflict between parents and teenagers. Many adolescents are not willing to wait for a gradual transfer of power as they develop in maturity, responsibility, and experience. They want to run things now. And often, they insist on sampling the adult vices that have been denied them.

Mothers and fathers face a terrible dilemma when this occurs. They must continue to lead their underaged children. That is their God-given responsibility as parents— and, it's the law of the land. But parents are limited in what they can force their kids to do. Furthermore, teenagers vary tremendously in their degree of maturity. Some sixteen-year-olds could handle independence and freedom. Others lacking supervision would wreck their lives in a matter of weeks. That sets up a terrible struggle that leaves everyone exhausted, hurt, and angry.

There are some approaches that have been successful in lessening this conflict. The religious group known as the Amish have developed a unique tradition that has succeeded for them. Their children are kept under very tight control when they are young. Strict discipline and harsh standards of behaviour are imposed from infancy. When children turn sixteen years of age, however, they enter a period called *Rumspringa*. Suddenly, all restrictions are lifted. They are free to drink, smoke, date, marry, or behave in ways that horrify their parents. Some do just that. But most don't. They are even granted the right to leave the Amish community if they choose. But if they stay, it must be in accordance with the social order. The majority accept the heritage of their families, not because they must, but because they choose to.

Although I admire the Amish and many of their approaches to child-rearing, I believe the Rumspringa concept is implemented too quickly for children raised in a more open society. To take a teenager overnight from rigid control to complete emancipation is an invitation to anarchy. It works in the controlled environment of Amish country, but it is usually disastrous for the rest of us. I've seen families grant 'instant adulthood' to their adolescents, to their regret. The result has been similar to what occurred in African colonies when European leadership was suddenly withdrawn. Bloody revolutions were often fought in the power vacuum that was created.

THE TRANSFER OF POWER

If it doesn't work to transfer power suddenly to young people, how can they be established as fully-fledged adults without creating a civil war in the process? I have recommended to your parents that they begin granting independence literally in toddlerhood. When a child can tie his shoes, he should be permitted—yes, required—to do it. When she can choose her clothes, she should make her own selections within reason. When he can walk safely to school, he should be allowed to do so. Each year, more responsibility and freedom (they are companions) must be given to the child so that the final release in early adulthood is merely a small, final release of authority. This is the theory, at least. Pulling it off is sometimes quite another matter.

For those of you who are critical of how your mum and dad have handled the transfer of power, I urge you to be charitable to them. It is extremely difficult to be good parents today. Even those who are highly motivated to do the job right often make a mess of things.

Why? Because children are infinitely complex. There is no formula that works in every case. In fact, I believe it is more difficult to raise children now than ever before. Be assured that you will not do the job perfectly, either. Someday, if you are blessed with children, one or more of them will blame you for your failures, just as you may have criticised your parents.

If there is tension within your family today, there are some things you can do to lessen it. The first is to leave home before you overstay your welcome. Many young adults in their early twenties hang around the house too long because they don't know what to do next. That is a recipe for trouble. Your mother and father can't help 'parenting' you if you remain under their noses. To them, it seems like only yesterday since you were born. They find it difficult to think of you as an adult.

The way you live probably irritates them, too. They hate your messy room, which would require a tetanus jab just to walk through. They don't like your music. They go to bed early and rise with the sun; you keep the same hours as hamsters. You drive the family car like you've been to Kamikaze Driving School. They want you to get a job—go to school—do *something*. Everyday brings a new argument—a new battle. When things deteriorate to that point, it's time to pack.

WHEN IS IT TIME TO LEAVE?

I visited a home several years ago where this battle was raging. The parents had posted a notice on the refrigerator that summed up their frustration. It said:

Their kids didn't take the hint. They were still there, watching daytime television and arguing over whose turn it was to take out the rubbish.

> *It is extremely difficult to be good parents today.*

The issue of when to leave home is of great importance to your future. Remaining too long under the 'parentos' roof is

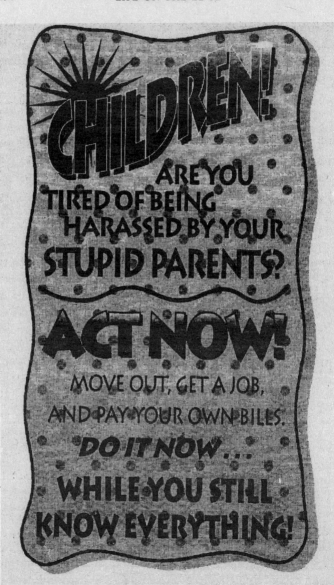

not unlike an unborn baby who refuses to leave the womb. It has every reason to stay awhile. It is warm and cozy there. All its needs are met in that stress-free environment. It doesn't have to work or study or discipline itself.

But it would be crazy to stay beyond the nine months God intended. It can't grow and learn without leaving the security of that place. Its development will be arrested until it enters the cold world and takes a few whacks on its behind. It is to everyone's advantage, and especially to the welfare of its mother, that the baby slides on down the birth canal and gets on with life.

> *Until you . . . begin providing for yourself, you will remain in a state of arrested development.*

So it is in young adulthood. Until you cut the umbilical cord and begin providing for yourself, you will remain in a state of arrested development. To use an earlier analogy, it is another of the 'mudholes' that can trap and hold a person in an immature state.

The Scripture hints at this need to press on. The apostle Paul wrote, 'When I was a child, I talked like a child, I thought like a child, I reasoned like a child. When I became a man, I put childish ways behind me' (1 Corinthians. 13:11). Remaining at home with Mum and Dad is the perpetuation of childhood. It may be time to put it behind you.

There is a variation on this theme that is even more problematical. It occurs when you have been away to attend college or to work, and then you've returned to live at home again. That is called 'the elastic nest', and it can be a disaster. Why? Because you've been on your own—you've made your own decisions and controlled your own life. You've changed dramatically during your time away, but you return to find that your parents have not. They are just as you left them. They want to tell you how to run your life—what to eat, what to wear, which friends to cultivate, etc. It is a formula for combat.

I understand that situation because I've been through it. My parents handled me wisely in my late teens, and it was rare for them to stumble into common parental mistakes. That is, however, exactly what happened when I was nineteen years old. We had been a very close-knit family, and it was difficult for my mother to change gear when I graduated from high school.

During that summer, I travelled 1,500 miles from home and entered a college in California. I will never forget the exhilarating feeling of freedom that swept over me that autumn. It was not that I wanted to do anything evil or forbidden. It was simply that I felt accountable for my own life and did not have to explain my actions to anyone. It was like a fresh, cool breeze on a spring morning. Young adults who have not been properly prepared for that moment sometimes go berserk, but I did not. I did, however, quickly become addicted to this freedom and was not about to give it up.

The following summer, I came home to visit my folks. Immediately, I found myself in conflict with my mum. She was not intentionally insulting. She simply responded as she had done a year earlier when I was still in high school. But by then, I had journeyed down the road towards independence. She was asking me what time I would be coming in at night and urging me to drive the car safely and advising me about what I ate. No offence was intended. My mother had just failed to notice that I had changed and she needed to get with the 'new programme'.

Finally, there was a flurry of words between us, and I left the house in a huff. A friend came by to pick me up, and I talked about my feelings as we rode in the car. 'Darn it, Bill!' I said. 'I don't need a mother anymore.'

Then a wave of guilt swept over me. It was as though I

had said, 'I don't love my mother anymore.' I meant no such thing. What I was feeling was a desire to be friends with my parents instead of accepting their authority over me. Freedom was granted very quickly thereafter.

I hope you will be a bit more patient with your parents than I was with mine. I was only nineteen years old, and I wanted it all. I should have given them another year to adjust. Your mum and dad will also change their thinking if you give them a little time. In the meanwhile, if you are twenty-two or older and have been away from home, I would suggest that you do not plan to return except for a specified period unless you have an unusually har-monious relationship with your parents. For most young people, bouncing back is built for trouble.

PARENTING IS LIKE . . .

To give you a better perspective on what your parents might be feeling today, consider this analogy: The task of raising children is rather like trying to fly a kite on a day when the wind doesn't blow. Mum and Dad run down the road pulling the cute little device at the end of a string. It bounces along the ground and shows no inclination of flying.

Eventually and with much effort, they manage to get it fifteen feet in the air, but great danger suddenly looms. The kite dives towards power lines and twirls near trees. It is a scary moment. Will they ever get it safely on its way? Then, unexpectedly, a gust of wind catches the kite, and it sails upwards while Mum and Dad feed out line as rapidly as they can.

The kite begins to pull the string, making it difficult to hold on. Inevitably, they reach the end of their line. What should they do now? The kite is demanding more freedom.

It wants to go higher. Dad stands on his tiptoes and raises his hand to accommodate the tug. It is now grasped tenuously between his index finger and thumb, held upwards towards the sky. Then the moment of release comes. The string slips through his fingers, and the kite soars majestically into God's beautiful sky.

The task of raising kids is rather like trying to fly a kite on a day when the wind doesn't blow.

Mum and Dad stand gazing at their precious 'baby' who is now gleaming in the sun, a mere pinpoint of colour on the horizon. They are proud of what they've done—but sad to realise that their job is finished. It was a labour of love. But where did the years go?

Not only is it healthy to understand what your parents are thinking during this 'letting-go' period, but I think you should also know what the future holds between you and them. The natural progression during a lifetime moves from authority in childhood to friendship during your adult years and finally to your parents' dependency on you as they age. Can you believe that? Those strong people on whom you have leaned will, if they live long enough, look to you eventually for strength and leadership. It is one of the most dramatic turnarounds that occurs in this human experience.

EVENTUALLY, THE ROLES WILL CHANGE

Writer and humorist Erma Bombeck described that transformation in her book *If Life Is a Bowl of Cherries, What Am I Doing in the Pits?* Included in that collection of writings was a short piece entitled, 'When Does the Mother Become the Daughter and the Daughter Become the Mother?' Erma begins by saying that her mother had always been strong, independent, and secure. She had attempted to model herself after this woman who had brought her into the world. But in recent years, Mum was changing. She was undeniably becoming more childlike.

Erma first noticed the change when they were riding in a car one day. She was driving and her mum was sitting near the right front door. Suddenly an emergency occurred, causing Erma to slam on the brakes. Instinctively, she reached out to keep her mother from hitting the windscreen. When the crisis had passed, the two women sat looking at one another. Each realised that something had changed in their relationship . . . for in prior years, Mum would have attempted to protect Erma.

Then there was the following Thanksgiving when Erma roasted the turkey and her mother set the table. Clearly, the mother was becoming the daughter, and the daughter was becoming the mother. As time passed, the transformation became more dramatic. When the two women were going shopping, it was Erma who said, 'My goodness, don't you look nice in that new dress,' and, 'Don't forget to wear your sweater so you won't get cold in the department stores.' Echoing in her mind was the advice of a concerned mother, 'Button up your coat, Erma. Wear your galoshes, stay warm, take care of yourself.'

Mrs Bombeck understood the new role she was asked to play but resisted it vigorously. She didn't want to see this strong, noble woman become dependent—childlike—insecure. Nevertheless, the inexorable march of time could not be resisted. She had to get her mother up at night to take her to the bathroom and to care for most of her physical needs. How different the relationship had become. When Erma was a kindergartner, she had made a plaster-of-Paris 'hand' that decorated the kitchen wall. Forty years later, mum was sent to a senior citizens' crafts class where she made a macramé. It eventually hung in her room at the Bombeck home.

As senility began to creep in, Erma found her own frustration rising to a crescendo. She said on one occasion, 'Mum, will you please stop talking about seeing Dad last night? You know he's been gone for ten years.' But Mum couldn't help it because she was no longer mentally competent. That completed the transformation. The mother had become the daughter, and the daughter had become the mother.

Shortly thereafter, Erma and her own daughter were riding in a car one day. There was a sudden breaking of cars, and the illumination of lights. Instinctively, the daughter reached out to protect Erma from hitting the windscreen. They looked at each other for a moment, and Erma said, 'My Lord! How quickly!' [8]

How quickly, indeed! One of the most wrenching experiences of the forties for me was watching my mother become my daughter and begin to look at me as her father. She eventually developed Parkinson's disease and went through the slow decline towards dependency and death. In the end, she was childlike in a way I would not have believed possible a few decades earlier.

BE PREPARED FOR INEVITABLE CHANGE

Why have I chosen to share this aspect of life with those of you who are young with parents still in the bloom of health? Because it may make you more tolerant now to understand that the power they hold is temporary. You won't always have to struggle to rid yourself of their authority. It will be handed to you. Even five more years will bring remarkable changes in your relationship.

Before you know it, their time will come to leave this world, if the probabilities hold true. You will then be left to carry on without them. And then, would you believe, one day you will become the 'son' or 'daughter' of your children, and they will become your 'parents'?

Let me speak candidly to those of you who have been most angry at your parents. Given the brevity of life and the temporary nature of all human relationships, can you find it within your hearts to forgive them? Perhaps my personal experience will speak to you. My mother closed her eyes for the last time on 26 June 1988, and went to be with the Lord. She had been so vibrant—so important to each member of our family. I couldn't imagine life without her just a few years earlier. But time passed so quickly, and before we knew it, she had grown old and sick and incompetent. This human experience is like that. In just a brief moment, it seems, our fleeting days are gone, and as King David said, 'The place thereof will know it no more.'

As I sat at the memorial service for my good mother, I was flooded with memories and a profound sense of loss. But there was not the slightest hint of regret, remorse, or guilt. There were no hurtful words I wished I could have taken back. There were no brawls—no prolonged conflicts—that remained unresolved between my parents and me.

Why not? Was I a perfect son, born to flawless parents? Of course not. But in 1962, when Shirley and I had been married two years and I was twenty-six years old, I remember saying to her, 'Our parents will not always be with us. I see now the incredible brevity of life that will someday take them from us. We *must* keep that in mind as we live out our daily lives. I want to respond to both sets of parents in such a way that we will have *no* regrets after they are gone. This is what I believe the Lord wants of us.'

> *One day you will become the 'son' or 'daughter' of your children.*

Again, to those of you who are in need of this advice, I urge you not to throw away these good, healthy times. Your parents will not always be there for you. Please think about what I have written and be careful not to create bitter memories that will hang above you when the record is in the books. No conflict is worth letting that happen.

I'll leave you with a powerful story by Sue Kidd that will make its own case. I hope you'll read it carefully. There's a message here for all of us:

DON'T LET IT END THIS WAY

The hospital was unusually quiet that bleak January evening, quiet and still like the air before a storm. I stood in the nurses' station on the seventh floor and glanced at the clock. It was 9.00 p.m.

I threw a stethoscope around my neck and headed for room 712, last room in the corridor. Room 712 had a new patient. Mr Williams. A man all alone. A man strangely silent about his family.

As I entered the room, Mr Williams looked up eagerly, but dropped his eyes when he saw it was only me, his nurse. I pressed the stethoscope over his chest and listened. Strong, slow, even beating. Just what I wanted to hear. There seemed little indication he had suffered a slight heart attack a few hours earlier.

He looked up from his starched white bed. 'Nurse, would you—' He hesitated, tears filling his eyes. Once before he had started to ask me a question, but had changed his mind.

I touched his hand, waiting.

He brushed away a tear. 'Would you call my daughter? Tell her I've had a heart attack. A slight one. You see, I live alone and she is the only family I have.' His respiration suddenly speeded up.

I turned his nasal oxygen up to eight litres a minute. 'Of course I'll call her,' I said, studying his face.

He gripped the sheets and pulled himself forwards, his face tense with urgency. 'Will you call her right away—as soon as you can?' He was breathing fast—too fast.

'I'll call her the very first thing,' I said, patting his shoulder.

I switched off the light. He closed his eyes, such young blue eyes in his fifty-year-old face.

Room 712 was dark except for a faint night light under the sink. Oxygen gurgled in the green tubes above his bed. Reluctant to leave, I moved through the shadowy silence to the window. The panes were cold. Below a foggy mist curled through the hospital car park.

'Nurse,' he called, 'could you get me a pencil and paper?'

I dug a scrap of yellow paper and a pen from my pocket and put it on the bedside table.

I walked back to the nurses' station and sat in a squeaky swivel chair by the phone. Mr Williams's daughter was listed on his chart as the next of kin. I got her number from information and dialled. Her soft voice answered.

'Janie, this is Sue Kidd, a registered nurse at the hospital. I'm calling about your father. He was admitted tonight with a slight heart attack and—'

'No!' she screamed into the phone, startling me. 'He's not dying is he?'

'His condition is stable at the moment,' I said, trying hard to sound convincing.

Silence. I bit my lip.

'You must not let him die!' she said. Her voice was so utterly compelling that my hand trembled on the phone.

'He is getting the very best care.'

'But you don't understand,' she pleaded. 'My daddy and I haven't spoken in almost a year. We had a terrible argument on my twenty-first birthday, over my boyfriend. I ran out of the house. I—I haven't been back. All these months I've wanted to go to him for forgiveness. The last thing I said to him was, "I hate you." '

Her voice cracked and I heard her heave great agonising sobs. I sat, listening, tears burning my eyes. A father and a daughter, so lost to each other. Then I was thinking of my own father, many miles away. It has been so long since I had said, 'I love you.'

As Janie struggled to control her tears, I breathed a prayer. 'Please God, let this daughter find forgiveness.'

'I'm coming. Now! I'll be there in thirty minutes,' she said. *Click.* She had hung up.

I tried to busy myself with a stack of charts on the desk. I couldn't concentrate. Room 712; I knew I had to get back to 712. I hurried down the hall nearly in a run. I opened the door.

Mr Williams lay unmoving. I reached for his pulse. There was none.

'Code 99, Room 712. Code 99. Stat'. The alert was speeding through the hospital within seconds after I called the switchboard through the intercom by the bed.

Mr Williams had had a cardiac arrest.

With lightning speed I levelled the bed and bent over his mouth, breathing air into his lungs. I positioned my hands over his chest and compressed. One, two, three. I tried to count. At fifteen I moved back to his mouth and breathed as deeply as I could. Where was help? Again I compressed and breathed. Compressed and breathed. He could not die!

'O God,' I prayed. 'His daughter is coming. Don't let it end this way.'

The door burst open. Doctors and nurses poured into the room pushing emergency equipment. A doctor took over the manual compression of the heart. A tube was inserted through his mouth as an airway. Nurses plunged syringes of medicine into the intravenous tubing.

I connected the heart monitor. Nothing. Not a beat. My own heart pounded. 'God, don't let it end like this. Not in bitterness and hatred. His daughter is coming. Let her find peace.'

'Stand back,' cried a doctor. I handed him the paddles for the electric shock to the heart. He placed them on Mr Williams's chest. Over and over we tried. But nothing. No response. Mr Williams was dead.

A nurse unplugged the oxygen. The gurgling stopped. One by one they left, grim and silent.

How could this happen? How? I stood by his bed, stunned. A cold wind rattled the window, pelting the panes with snow.

Outside—everywhere—seemed a bed of blackness, cold and dark. How could I face his daughter?

When I left the room, I saw her against the wall by a water fountain. A doctor who had been inside 712 only moments before stood at her side, talking to her, gripping her elbow. Then he moved on, leaving her slumped against the wall.

Such pathetic hurt reflected from her face. Such wounded eyes. She knew. The doctor had told her that her father was gone.

I took her hand and led her into the nurses' lounge. We sat on little green stools, neither saying a word. She stared straight ahead at a pharmaceutical calendar, glass-faced, almost breakable-looking.

'Janie, I'm so, so sorry,' I said. It was pitifully inadequate.

'I never hated him, you know. I loved him,' she said.

God, please help her, I thought.

Suddenly she whirled toward me. 'I want to see him.'

My first thought was, *Why put yourself through more pain? Seeing him will only make it worse.* But I got up and wrapped my arm around her. We walked slowly down the corridor to 712. Outside the door I squeezed her hand, wishing she would change her mind about going inside. She pushed open the door.

We moved to the bed, huddled together, taking small steps in unison. Janie leaned over the bed and buried her face in the sheets.

I tried not to look at her at this sad, sad good-bye. I backed against the bedside table. My hand fell upon a scrap of yellow paper. I picked it up. It read:

> *My dearest Janie,*
>
> *I forgive you. I pray you will also forgive me. I know that you love me. I love you too.*
> > > > > > > > > *Daddy*

The note was shaking in my hands as I thrust it towards

Janie. She read it once. Then twice. Her tormented face grew radiant. Peace began to glisten in her eyes. She hugged the scrap of paper to her breast.

'Thank You, God,' I whispered, looking up at the window. Crystal stars blinked through the blackness. A snow flake hit the window and melted away, gone forever.

Life seemed as fragile as a snowflake on the window. But thank You, God, that relationships, sometimes fragile as snowflakes, can be mended together again—but there is not a moment to spare.

I crept from the room and hurried to the phone. I would call my father. I would say, 'I love you'.[9]

QUESTIONS FROM THE EDGE

1. My dad is going through a major midlife crisis. At least that's what my mum says about him. Can you explain this to me? Why is he kind of going crazy at this time?

Well, I'll describe a typical midlife crisis, although every individual is unique and every case is different. The man in this mess is likely to be in his forties, but it could be earlier or later. He has worked very hard all his adult life but he's become bored with his job. He is keenly aware that he can't afford to leave or take a lower-paying position. Too many people are depending on him—not only his wife and teenage son and daughter, but also his own aging parents, too. His marriage has been unexciting for years, and he's begun wishing he could get out of it.

Another major influence on this man is his age. For the first time in his life, he's noticing that the sand is running out of the hourglass. He realises that the best years may be behind him and he's going to be old before very long. He begins to feel a kind of panic. Perhaps the best word to describe what this man is feeling is *trapped*. Life is passing him by, and he's stuck in a monotonous existence with no way out.

Right at that critical moment, a young, exciting woman may come along. She is probably a divorcée who is lonely and has needs of her own. She senses his restlessness and finds it enticing. He is very flattered by the attention she gives him. He feels young and virile when he's with her, and he begins thinking unthinkable thoughts. *Maybe, just maybe* . . . A whole new world beckons him, one filled with lust, freedom, and escape.

I counselled such a man who 'dumped' his wife and four children and resigned from an outstanding job. When I asked him why, he said, 'I had given my entire life to others, and quite frankly, fun and games looked good to me.'

This description of the turmoil behind a midlife crisis is written from a man's point of view, but I don't want you to misunderstand me. His behaviour is not justified, and in fact, it is a disaster for everyone concerned. He wounds his children, tears out his wife's heart, and usually destroys his own life. Because God will not tolerate sinful behaviour, the man frequently throws over his faith and charts a new course. He has just made the biggest mistake of his life even though he may not yet know it.

I certainly hope your father is not going down this road. You and the rest of the family need to pray that his eyes will be opened before it is too late. And your mother should read *Love Must Be Tough*.

2. **My friend is sixteen years old, and she is very rebellious. She got so mad at her parents this year that she ran away from home. I got a letter from her, and she's living on the streets in Hollywood. It sounds like she's doing OK, but I sure wish she'd come home. I don't even know**

how to contact her or I'd try to talk her into making up with her parents. They're really nice people.

Your friend probably does not realise what an enormous risk she is taking. I saw a report recently that indicated just how dangerous that lifestyle is. It showed that sixty-two per cent of underage girls who live on the streets die before their eighteenth birthday[10], Isn't that tragic? They are either murdered, commit suicide, die of disease, or fatally overdose on drugs. I wish every teenager, and especially every teenage girl, knew of the danger lurking in the city. It's better to stay home and try to work things out rather than subject themselves to the horrors of an early death.

3. You talked about music and its influence on my generation. It caused a different kind of problem for me. I've been having trouble hearing in one ear, and I went to a doctor to find out why. He put me through a bunch of tests and then told me that I have damaged my hearing by listening to so much loud music—especially when wearing a headset like a Walkman. I've been doing that ever since I was a preschooler, but no one ever told me that that could be damaging. Could you comment on that?

You've learned something rather late that you should have been told when you were younger. Our hearing apparatus is a mechanical instrument, dependent on three little bones in the middle ear. These delicate parts work together to transmit vibrations to the eardrum where they are then perceived as sound. Like any mechanical device, however, this apparatus is subject to wear. Therefore, those who live in a noisy environment, including those who keep a headset blaring in their ears, are continually operating those delicate parts and are gradually decreasing their hearing acuity.

A study was conducted of natives living in a quiet village within an isolated Amazon rain forest. They rarely heard noises louder than a squawking parrot or the sounds of children laughing and playing. Not surprisingly, their hearing remained almost perfect even into old age. There was virtually no deafness known to the tribe.

By contrast, people living in modern industrial societies are subject to the continual bombardment of noise pollution. Motorcycles, refuse trucks, television, and high-powered machines pound their ears from morning till night. Young people are particularly at risk because of their music. Attending a Rolling Stones concert is equivalent to being strapped to the bottom of a jet aeroplane that is taking off, or like being tied to the bonnet of a 'Mack' truck going sixty miles an hour.

Singer Pete Townshend, lead singer of the legendary rock group The Who is almost totally deaf in one ear from playing too close to electronic amplifiers and huge speakers for many years. He issued a warning to those who like their music loud. 'Someday, people will regret the unnecessary wear and tear on their hearing mechanism. We only have one body, and we must help it serve us for a lifetime.'

Like a ninety-year-old man said recently, 'If I'd have known I was gonna live so long I'd have taken better care of myself.'

4. Would you ever, under any circumstances, permit your son or daughter to bring a room-mate of the opposite sex to visit or to live?

No. That would be dishonouring God and a violation of the moral principles on which Shirley and I have staked our lives. I would bend for my kids, but never that far.

10

EMOTIONS: FRIEND OR FOE?

CHAPTER TEN

In the autumn of 1969, a wild man named Charles Manson and his young followers, known as 'the family', went on a bloody rampage in the city of Los Angeles. They killed actress Sharon Tate, who was nine months pregnant, and four or five other innocent people. A few nights later, they broke into the home of Leno and Rosemary LaBianca and butchered them in cold blood. Millions of people in that area read about these murders and were paralysed with fear. Neighbours wondered who would be next. My mother was convinced she was the prime candidate.

Sure enough, Mum and Dad were confronted by an intruder as they lay in bed one night. They heard a loud *Thump!* coming from the other side of the house.

'Did you hear that?' whispered my mother.

'Yes, be quiet,' said my father.

They lay staring at the darkened ceiling, breathing shallowly and listening for confirmation that someone was indeed there. A second *Thump* brought them to their feet. They felt their way to the bedroom door, which was closed. At this point, we see a striking difference in the way my mother and father faced a crisis. Her inclination was to hold the door shut to keep the intruder from entering their bedroom. Thus, she braced herself against the door and wedged her foot at the bottom. My father's approach was to confront the attacker head-on. He reached through the darkness and grasped the doorknob, but his pull met the resistance from my mother.

My father assumed someone was holding the door from the other side while my mother could feel the killer trying to force it open. My parents stood there in the blackness of midnight, struggling against one another and imagining themselves to be in a tug-of-war with a murderer. Mum then panicked. She ran to the window to scream for help. As she took in a great breath of air with which to summon the entire city of Los Angeles, she realised a light was on behind her. Turning around, she saw that my dad had gone into the other part of the house in search of their attacker. Obviously, he was able to open the door when she released it. As they discovered, there was no prowler in their house. The thumps were never identified, and Charles Manson was soon apprehended in Los Angeles and sent to prison for life.

EMOTIONS CAN DECEIVE

This story illustrates the way emotions sometimes deceive us. They are inveterate liars that will often confirm our worst fears in the absence of supporting evidence. Even the young and the brave can be fooled by the shenanigans of runaway emotions.

My friend Steve Smith would agree. He won a Bronze Star for courage in Vietnam, but the first night his unit was on the battlefield would not be remembered for its valour. His company had never seen actual combat, and the men were very uneasy. They dug foxholes on a hill as they nervously watched the sun disappear beyond the horizon. At approximately midnight, the enemy attacked with a vengeance. Guns began to blaze on one side of the mountain, and before long, all the soldiers were firing frantically and throwing hand grenades into the darkness.

The battle raged throughout the night, and the infantry appeared to be winning. At last, the long-awaited sun came up, and the body count began. But not one single dead Vietcong lay at the perimeter of the mountain. In fact, the enemy had not even participated in the attack. Their presence had been imagined by the nervous troops. They had engaged the night in mortal combat—and won!

Even the young and the brave can be foiled by the shenanigans of runaway emotions.

What causes normal, intelligent people to act in irrational ways when facing a perceived danger or threat? Why do so many of us 'go to pieces' when the chips are down? This tendency to panic results from the malfunction of a system known as the 'fight-or-flight' mechanism. That is a neurochemical process designed to prepare us for action whenever we face an immediate crisis. When we are frightened or stressed, adrenaline and other hormones are released that put our entire body on an alarm-reaction status. Our blood pressure is elevated, we become stronger and more alert, the pupils of our eyes dilate to gather more light, etc.

It is a very helpful mechanism when it functions properly. But when it runs amok, an individual can behave in very strange ways. You call that 'freaking out'. We call it 'hysteria', and it can grip large numbers of people simultaneously.

In 1973 a strange illness swept through a junior high school in the community of Berry, Alabama. Within a period of about three hours, more than one hundred students and teachers experienced intense itching, fainting, stomach aches, tingling fingers, and other symptoms. Seventy people were treated in the emergency ward of a nearby hospital. Health department officials rushed to investigate the puzzling epidemic. They considered the possibility of poisons, infections, or even allergies that would explain the illness. They checked out reports of crop dusters spraying insecticides near the school and rumors of chemicals being stolen from the National Guard Armoury. No stone was left unturned in their effort to identify the source of the suffering.

Soon, Dr Frederick Wolf, Alabama state epidemiologist, announced that they had found no cause for the illness. 'There was simply nothing found,' he said.

'We checked everything,' said an epidemic intelligence officer from the Alabama State Department of Health.

A MYSTERIOUS DISEASE . . .
COMPLETE WITH SYMPTOMS

So what caused the symptoms that afflicted so many people simultaneously? The researchers concluded it was hysteria, plain and simple. The students and teachers were victims of their own imaginations, which made them think they were sick when they were not. It is a very common phenomenon.[1]

My concern is not only about hysteria and other types of irrational fear but the problem with our emotions themselves. Much of the time they are not to be believed. I wouldn't deny the importance of feelings or the role they play in our humanness. Indeed, those who have so insulated themselves that they no longer feel are very unhealthy individuals.

In the 1993 movie *Shadowlands,* writer C. S. Lewis loved a woman who died prematurely. Her death was intensely painful to him, causing Lewis to question whether he should have permitted himself to care for her. He concluded in the last scene that we are given two choices in life. We can allow ourselves to love and care for others, which makes us vulnerable to their sickness, death, or rejection. Or we can protect ourselves by refusing to love. Lewis decided that it is better to feel and to suffer than to go through life isolated, insulated, and lonely. I agree strongly.

I am not recommending, therefore, that we build walls to protect ourselves from pain. But we must understand that emotions are unreliable and at times, tyrannical. They should never be permitted to dominate us. That principle was generally understood in our culture for hundreds of years. During the revolutionary days of the late sixties, however, a major shift in attitude occurred, especially among the young. One of the popular notions of the day was, 'If it feels good, do it'. That phrase says it all. It means that a person's flighty impulses should be allowed to overrule every other consideration—including the needs of children, principles of right and wrong, a person's long-term goals, lurking dangers, and common sense. 'Don't think—just follow your heart', was the prevailing attitude.

That is damnable advice. It has ruined many gullible people. Behaviour has consequences, and stupid behaviour often has terrible consequences. If you follow blindly the dictates of emotion instead of controlling them with your will and intellect, you are casting yourself adrift in the path of life's storms.

> *We must understand that emotions are unreliable and at times, tyrannical.*

I once wrote a book whose title asked this question: *Emotions: Can You Trust Them?* It took me two hundred pages to say, 'No!' Emotions are biased—whimsical—unreliable. They lie as often as they tell the truth. They are manipulated by hormones—especially in the teen years—and they wobble from early morning, when we are rested, to the evening, when we are tired.

One of the evidences of emotional maturity is the ability (and the willingness) to overrule ephemeral feelings and govern our behaviour with reason. This might lead you to 'tough it out' when you feel like escaping—and guard your tongue when you feel like shouting—and to save your money when you feel like spending it—and to remain faithful when you feel like flirting—and to put the welfare of others above your own. These are mature acts that can't occur when feelings are in charge.

WE MUST TAKE CHARGE OF OUR EMOTIONS

The Scriptures instruct us to subjugate our emotions and make them dance to our tune. Well, they say approximately that. We read in 2 Corinthians 10:5, '. . .we take captive every thought to make it obedient to Christ'. That's pretty clear isn't it? Consider Galatians 5:22, 'But when the Holy Spirit controls our lives he will produce this kind of fruit in us: love, joy, peace, patience, kindness, goodness, faithfulness, gentleness and self-control' (TLB). These are called 'the fruits of the Spirit', and they begin with the attribute listed last—the exercise of self-control.

We also need to understand how emotions influence us and the principles by which they work. First, it is helpful to know that they are cyclical in nature. There is a certain rhythm to our mental apparatus. Haven't you noticed from your own experience that highs are followed by lows and lows

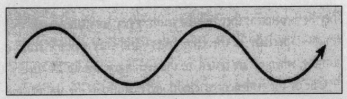

by highs? The reason is that there is a regular fluctuation, almost like a mathematical sine curve (illustrated below), that takes us systematically from a peak of enthusiasm to a mild depression. In women, that pattern generally follows the phases of the menstrual cycle. In men, it is more environmental in origin. But it exists for both genders.

Not only are emotions cyclical, but each person has their own characteristic 'wobble'. In other words, individual personalities do not extend much further up than they do down. If we draw a line through the curve symbolising the emotional centre (neither high nor low), the distance from there to the peak for a particular person is usually the same as the distance from there to the valley.

I'll explain what I mean by looking at temperaments representing the two extremes. Type 1 people, as illustrated below, don't get very excited about anything. These Steady Eddies and Stable Mabels don't cheer very loudly at football games, and their laughter is never boisterous. Good news is received about as calmly as bad.

On the other hand, they never get very depressed, either. They are rather dull people, but at least they are consistently dull! You can count on them to be the same yesterday, today, and tomorrow. If a husband comes home and announces he's taking his wife to Hawaii or Paris for a holiday, this Type 1 lady will probably smile and say, 'Fine.' And the new Porsche in the driveway won't thrill her either. That's just the way she is made. Her emotional pattern looks like this:

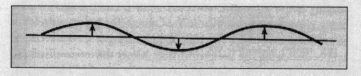

By contrast, Type 2 people (depicted over) are the world's

true 'swingers'. Their emotions bounce from the rafters down to the basement and back up the wall again.

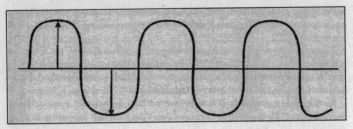

We all know at least one Type 2 individual who gets extremely happy every now and then. They rise in the morning and giggle at the very thought of the sunrise. They wave at the birds and grin at the flowers and whistle zippity-doo-dah throughout the day. Beware of this type! I guarantee you they are going to crash and burn in a few days.

When that come-down occurs, despair will settle on their head. Nothing will go right, life won't be worth living, they will have no friends, and woe will fill the entire earth. They are so sentimental they'll weep at supermarket openings. They are truly an emotional yo-yo. And for reasons I've never been able to explain, this Type 2 extremist will probably marry a Type 1 bore, and the two of them will irritate each other for the rest of their lives.

My wife and I attended a symphony in Berlin during our first trip to Europe. Sitting in front of us was a young man who was probably studying music at a local university. He went into some kind of strange ecstasy during the first half of the performance, swaying to the orchestration with his eyes closed and standing to cheer after every number. Following the last performance before the intermission, he went almost out of his mind with delight. You would have thought he'd just won the Grand National. He yelled, 'Bravo! Bravo!' and waved to the conductor.

But wouldn't you know, the second half of the performance made him sick. He slumped in his chair, booed the orchestra, and muttered his displeasure throughout the remaining hour of the concert. He finally sprang to his feet and pushed towards the aisle, stepping on toes, knees, and Beethoven's Fifth Symphony, stalking from the auditorium in a huff.

Though I've never seen this young man either before or after the performance, it is obvious that he was a Type 2 personality. His capacity to experience a 'high' in the first half was matched by an equal and opposite 'low' a few minutes later.

Frankly, I enjoyed his antics more than I did the music, but I wouldn't want him as a brother-in-law. You can bet *everything* is a big deal to him.

WHAT GOES UP MUST COME DOWN

Now let's address another aspect of our cyclical emotions. It is important to understand that anything that takes you up will also bring you down, and vice versa. For example, mild depression is likely to appear following a busy holiday, the birth of a baby, a job promotion, or even after a restful holiday. The cause for it is physical in nature. Elation and excitement are driven by adrenaline, which results in a greater consumption of energy. After a few days in that hyper-state, there has to be a come-down. If you understand that mechanism, you can brace yourself for the low end of the cycle.

That is what happened to Shirley and me when we bought a new house some years ago. We had waited for years to find a home we could afford, and we became very excited when contracts were exchanged and it was finally ours. The elation lasted for several days, during which I thought about this cyclical principle. I remember telling

Shirley we could not remain elated much longer. We needed to prepare ourselves for the lower end of the curve.

Sure enough, we both became mildly depressed in a couple of days. It wasn't a severe reaction, just a case of what some people call 'the blues'. The house didn't seem so wonderful, and we worried about the price we had paid for it.

Anything that takes you up will also bring you down, and vice versa.

We lived there for nineteen years and grew to love the place, but we thought we had made a mistake during our brief moment in 'the pits'.

Your own occasional depression will be more tolerable if you understand it as a relatively predictable occurrence. Highs *must* be followed by lows. It is governed by a physical law; you can depend on it. But in the healthy individual, lows eventually give way to highs, too. It cuts both ways.

There is another characteristic of these mood swings that should be especially useful to those who are married or plan to get married. Since romantic love is an emotion, it conforms to the same cyclical pattern I have described. You already know that the excitement of a new love affair is like nothing else in human experience. A couple in that relationship enter into a kind of ecstasy that is almost indescribable. *This is it! The search is over!* They've found the perfect human being. They want to be together twenty-four hours a day—to take walks in the rain and sit by the fire and kiss and cuddle. Hooray for love!

What too few couples know, unfortunately, is that tl exhilarating feeling **Never** lasts very long. As with otl temporary moods and feelings, it is destined from t beginning to swing down from that high and hit ro bottom. It is absolutely inevitable! Thus, if you ident genuine love with that feeling, you're going to be very cc... fused when it passes. This is the tender trap that leads many young people to make a disastrous mistake. The romantic excitement between them feels like something they can live on forever. Then . . . it goes away, sometimes on the honeymoon or maybe a few months later.

I'm not implying that such a couple are no longer in love. I am saying that the romantic feeling they shared is not love. It sometimes precedes the real thing. Genuine love is much deeper and more stable. It is based on a commitment of the will, a determination to make it work, and the bonding I described earlier. With these elements in place, a relationship can be as steady and predictable as the sunrise. Meanwhile, the feeling will continue to come and go throughout their married life.

I was trying to explain this up-and-down characteristic to a group of one hundred young married couples to whom I was speaking. During the discussion that followed, someone asked one guy why he and his wife married so young. He replied, ' 'Cause I didn't know about that wiggly line until it was too late.' For the rest of you, there is no excuse. You now understand that feelings will not carry a relationship very far. Feelings are important, to be sure, but they must be supported by the will and a lifetime commitment.

SO WHERE ARE ALL THESE MOUNTAIN TOPS?

This point is so important that I must emphasise it. If you expect to live for months or years on a romantic mountain top, you can forget it. You won't stay there. My concern is for the many naïve young couples who 'fall in love' and lock themselves into marriage early in the relationship before the natural swing of their emotions has even had its first dip. They then waken one morning without that great feeling and conclude that love has died. In reality, it was never there in the first place. They were fooled by an emotional high before it came sliding downwards. This is the bottom line:

If you expect to live for months or years on a romantic mountain top, you can forget it.

When love is defined as a feeling, the relationship can be no more stable than a frame of mind.

Remember that the greatest passage ever written about love, recorded in 1 Corinthians 13, does not even mention feelings. It tells us:

> Love is patient, love is kind. It does not envy, it does not boast, it is not proud. It is not rude, it is not self-seeking, it is not easily angered, it keeps no record of wrongs. Love does not delight in evil but rejoices with the truth. It always protects, always trusts, always hopes, always perseveres. Love never fails (1 Corinthians. 13:4–8).

That sets the record straight.

There is a related matter that I feel we must touch, at least, before concluding. Our spiritual lives also conform to the characteristics I have described. Many people who repent of their sins and become followers of Jesus Christ subsequently experience the kind of 'honeymoon' that is typical for romantic lovers.

They feel an incredible sense of cleanness and harmony with God. It is not unusual for such new converts to read the Bible many times each day and to think about little else. Those individuals are in danger of spiritual confusion, because once again, their feelings will be temporary. Emotions cannot remain supercharged, even for the noblest reasons.

As with romantic love, our relationship with the Lord goes through distinct emotional stages. First there is the courtship, when we are getting to know Him and beginning to understand His holy Word. Then there is the honeymoon period, which is nothing short of exhilarating. Finally, there is the steady, deep, but less-emotional experience of married life. This third stage is marked by a quiet commitment and growing maturity as the years unfold.

New believers who don't understand how emotions change in time may become disillusioned and conclude that their faith is meaningless. It is a tragic mistake. Their relationship with the Lord must be based on Scripture and its claims, rather than linking it to ephemeral feelings that blow hot and cold. You can be as close to the Lord when you feel nothing as when you're in the grip of spiritual passion.

I've addressed this topic in greater detail in my book *Emotions: Can You Trust Them?* It is relevant here because of the need for self-awareness when we are young. Socrates gave that advice to each of his students 2,500 years ago when he instructed them to 'Know thyself'. That has been the goal of this brief discussion.

We began with a story about my mother. We'll end with another. She attended a small-town high school in Oklahoma during the 1930s that had produced a series of terrible football teams. They usually lost the big games and were invariably clobbered by their archrivals from a nearby community. Understandably, the students and their parents began to feel depressed and dispirited by the drubbing their troops were given every Friday night. It must have been awful.

> *You can be as close to the Lord when you feel nothing as when you're in the grip of spiritual passion.*

Finally, a local automobile dealer decided to take matters into his own hands. He asked to speak to the team in the locker room after yet another devastating defeat. What followed was one of the most dramatic football speeches of all times. This businessman proceeded to offer a brand new Ford to every boy on the team and to each coach if they would simply defeat their bitter rivals in the next game.

The team went crazy with anticipation. They howled and cheered and slapped each other on their padded shoulders. For seven days, the boys ate, drank, and breathed football. At night they dreamed about touchdowns and 'rumbleseats'. The entire school caught the spirit of ecstasy, and a holiday fever pervaded the campus. Each player could visualise himself behind the wheel of a sleek roadster with eight or ten gorgeous girls hanging all over his body.

Finally, the big night arrived and the team assembled in the locker room. Excitement was at an unprecedented high. The coach offered several last-minute instructions, and the boys hurried out to face the enemy. They assembled on the sidelines, put their hands together, and shouted a simultaneous 'Rah!' Then they ran onto the field—and were demolished, thirty-eight to nil.

All their exuberance didn't translate into a single point on the scoreboard. Seven days of hoorah and whoop-de-do simply couldn't compensate for the players' lack of discipline, conditioning, practice, study, coaching, drill, experience, and character. Such is the nature of emotion. It has a definite place in human affairs. But it must always be ruled by the higher mental faculties of will and intellect. When left to stand alone, feelings usually reveal themselves to be unreliable and even a bit foolish.

So enjoy the exhilaration when it comes. Take the ride to the heights when you get the opportunity. But don't get hooked on the thrill of the moment. Take charge of your emotions. And when its time to do the right thing, don't let your feelings lead you to compromise. That is the way to live a happier, more successful life and one that is more pleasing to God.

QUESTIONS FROM THE EDGE

1. Sometimes I feel like the world is stacked against me. I'm not sure why, except I just think I don't have a chance to really be somebody. Whenever something goes wrong for me, I say to myself, *What did you expect? It always happens that way.* Do other people feel like I do?

Yes, many people have that attitude. They, like you, see themselves as 'victims' who are destined to come out on the short-end of things. It is a common reaction, especially among people with a disability and among those who don't like the way they look, by those who were abused as children, etc.

But the problem has become even broader in recent years. Our society is telling us that we're all victims of some sort of abuse. Hispanics, African-Americans, Asians, Jews, Native Americans, women, children, and now even white males are supposed to feel discriminated against. Yes, discrimination and racism are still serious problems in today's society, but it doesn't help to make us all feel like we're being 'had' in one way or another. The net effect of this mind-set is to fracture us into competing special interest groups, instead of binding us together in unity. I call it 'the curse of universal victimisation'.

Let me speak very candidly to those of you who believe the world is out to get you. What you're feeling is a form of self-hatred, which is very destructive. It is also demoralising. Whenever you begin to conclude, 'I can't win', and 'What's the use?' you've set yourself up for failure. Your pessimism becomes a kind of self-fulfilling prophecy. It doesn't have to be that way.

Let me tell you a story about my friend David Hernandez. His parents were illegal immigrants from Mexico who were trying to start a new life in this country.

Unfortunately, they couldn't find work for months, and the children were hungry for weeks at a time. Finally, the family was hired as migrant farmworkers to harvest the potato crop in the state of California. They lived under trees and used an oil drum as a stove. They owned nothing and had very little chance of escaping the suffocating grip of poverty.

Despite their depressing circumstances, the Hernandez family had a certain dignity and strength about them. They were Christians, and they taught their children that God loved them and had a plan for their lives. Their little boy, David, internalised that message of hope. He never thought of himself as a victim even though he had every reason to feel cheated. His family was at the bottom of the social ladder without even a house to live in, but his worth as an individual was rooted in his faith.

David began attending state schools, and he proved to be an outstanding student. As he grew older, he was given a scholarship to attend a private school where he continued to excel academically. To make a long story short, he went on to graduate from college near the top of his class and was granted admission to Loma Linda University School of Medicine. He earned his medical degree and went into a surgical residency in obstetrics and gynaecology. Dr David Hernandez then became a professor at both Loma Linda University and the University of Southern California schools of medicine.

Whenever you begin to conclude, 'I can't win,' and 'What's the use?' you've set yourself up for failure.

Who would have thought that the little Mexican boy in the potato fields would become a highly respected physician and medical teacher? It would never have happened if David had seen himself as a helpless victim—a loser whom life had 'short-changed'. Because he refused to adopt a defeatist attitude, he overcame the obstacles in his path.

But life was to deal David Hernandez yet another challenge. He called one day to tell me that he had been diagnosed with a terrible liver disease. He was still in his thirties at the time. A few years later David died from this rare disorder called sclerosing cholangitis.

I went to see him in the hospital a few days before the end. Though very sick, David did not whine or ask, 'Why me?' Even in that difficult hour when he knew death was imminent, he never indulged in self-pity. He knew intuitively that a person is only a victim if he accepts himself as one.

> *Resist the temptation to see yourself as a victim.*

I strongly advise you to follow Dr David Hernandez's model—to resist the temptation to see yourself as a victim. Fight it with all your might. It is one of Satan's most powerful weapons against you, and it is a lie. God made you with His own hands, and He doesn't make junk. He will help you overcome the circumstances that present themselves as obstacles lying in your path.

2. My former girlfriend and I thought we were madly in love because we were crazy about each other from the moment we met. We were together every day and all our friends thought we would get married. But the relationship cooled off very quickly and now we can hardly stand each other. I don't even like to be around her. What do you think happened to us?

Not knowing either of you, it is difficult to say for sure. But I can tell you that the way your relationship began had something to do with the way it ended. As I've indicated, a love affair is usually doomed when it begins with great intensity. It usually burns itself out in time. In a manner of speaking, you and your girlfriend ran your race together as though it were a one-hundred-yard dash. It should have been approached like a marathon. That's why you exhausted yourselves before your journey together ever got started.

If a love relationship is to go the distance, there needs to be comfortable pacing that keeps the two parties from consuming each other. That will give the bond a chance to form—and allow the 'glue to dry'. Remember?

3. Is there a time of day when it's best to handle threatening or unpleasant topics?

There certainly is, and it is important to consider. Most of us cope with frustration much better in the morning than we do later in the day. It stands to reason that stressful topics are more difficult to handle when we are tired than when we are fresh. That's why I recommend that husbands and wives, and single individuals as well, do not talk about unpleasant topics at night. Most of our concerns will wait until morning when they will be less likely to upset us and create interpersonal crises.

11

THE HALLWAY OF DOORS

CHAPTER ELEVEN

I have referred several times to the many 'mudholes' that can trap and disable young adults during their journey through the critical decade. Now let me approach this theme from a different angle. For purposes of illustration, think of yourself as a teenager being required to walk alone down a long, dark corridor.

Low-wattage bulbs hang from the ceiling, casting eerie shadows on the walls. On either side of this hallway are many large doors, each bearing a different inscription. They are called Alcohol, Marijuana, Hard Drugs, Pornography, Gambling, Homosexual Experimentation, Premarital Sex, and so on. Every form of addictive behaviour is represented by at least one door. So there you are, groping along in the darkness and wondering what to do next. Should you stay on the straight and narrow—or push open one of the enticing doors?

As you approach each portal, you can hear boisterous laughter and gaiety coming from within. Your friends—or people you want as friends—are already inside, and they are obviously having a ball. Every now and then you hear someone call your name and ask you to join the party. Who knows what excitement awaits those with the courage to enter?

Slivers of light escaping from under each door reveal dancing bodies inside. Pounding music reverberates through the walls. As you stand there in the shadows, you ask yourself, *Why shouldn't I get in on the fun? Who has the right to shut me out?*

That does it! You reach for the doorknob.

What happens next could be remembered for a lifetime. Why? Because for a certain percentage of the individuals who open the doors, a tragedy begins to unfold. Lifelong addictions can be traced to that moment. Please understand I am not saying that every person who takes a drink or uses marijuana or places a bet at the racecourse will become addicted. It can be said, however, that some people are very vulnerable to certain chemicals and specific psychological needs. Repeated exposure when they are young will set them on the road to destructive patterns.

BROKEN DREAMS AND EMPTY PROMISES

I knew an older man who had made precisely this mistake in his youth. He was an alcoholic for most of his adult life. His inability to control his drinking and the violence it caused eventually destroyed his home, ruined his life, and wounded everyone he loved. He died a lonely and regretful man with very little to show for his seventy-seven years on this earth. How did it happen?

Did he plan to waste his wages each week and terrorise his little family? Did he intend to make his children fear him and drive his wife away? Was that his desire? Of course not. He promised a thousand times to stop drinking. But he was hooked. He couldn't stop. I'm sure as a young man he never dreamed he had the chemistry and temperament of an alcoholic. All he did was open a door that should have remained shut, and the rest is history.

I repeat, there is a percentage of the population that is

vulnerable to each potential addiction. Those in a high-risk category usually don't know it. When they open the wrong door, a monster rushes out and grabs them. Some will be held in its power for the rest of their lives.

You've probably seen it happen. You may be the child of an alcoholic or a compulsive gambler. Other readers may have had friends who experimented with 'crack' or 'speed' or heroin and are still struggling to free themselves from bondage. It happens every day.

There is a percentage of the population that is vulnerable to each potential addiction.

Addictions don't always result from chemical dependency such as drugs or alcohol. Some have a psychological origin, but they are just as captivating and destructive. Pornography, for example, is every bit as addictive to some teenage boys as cocaine. Exposure at the wrong time can capture a susceptible kid and pull them into a habit that lasts a lifetime.

Like most other addictions, the need for pornography is progressive in nature. It gets worse with the passage of time. Erotic photographs and videos quickly lose their power to stimulate. The viewer wants to see more and harder stuff! Sooner or later, they come to the end of the line—where they have seen everything a man and woman can do together. They have viewed the human body from every angle until it is no longer erotic to them. What then?

For a percentage of men hooked on porn, they will zoom past this natural barrier and develop an interest in perverse behaviour. They will lust for the most wretched material on earth, including depictions of child molestation, simulated murder, homosexual violence, sex between women and animals, sex with the dead, spreading excrement on the body, etc.

How can a person get excited over such unthinkably vile

material? It usually results from an early addiction to soft-core pornography that progresses, *for some individuals,* to the worst possible conclusion. The monster has claimed another victim.

All addictions eventually become a family affair. Pornography is no exception. It often destroys sex in marriage because men become hooked on a way that their wives usually resist. That creates terrible fights between them. He wants her to do things that repel her. Also, visual images and masturbation become a substitute for sexual relations between a husband and wife.

Air-brushed photographs of beautiful models and professionally produced videos make the real thing seem boring by comparison. Finally, females of all ages are commonly depicted in pornographic material being raped, tortured, and exploited sexually, which contributes to violence against women in real life.

A ROAD THAT LEADS TO NOWHERE

Ted Bundy understood that danger. When he was thirteen years old, he discovered some 'dirty magazines' on a rubbish tip near his home. He was instantly captivated by them. In time, Bundy became more and more addicted to violent images in magazines and videos. He got his kicks from seeing women being tortured and murdered. When he tired of this, there was only one place his addiction could go—from fantasy to reality.

Bundy, a good-looking, intelligent law student, learned to lure women into his car by various forms of deception. He would put a cast on his arm or leg, then walk across a university campus carrying several books. When he saw an interesting student standing or walking alone, he'd 'accidentally' drop the books near her. The girl would help him gath-

er them and take them to his car. Then he would entice her
or push her into the vehicle where she was taken captive.
After he had molested the girl and the rage of passion had
passed, she would be killed and Bundy would dump her
body in a region where it would not be found for months.
This went on for years.

By the time he was apprehended, Bundy had killed at
least twenty-eight young women and girls in acts too horrible to contemplate. He was finally convicted and sentenced to death for killing a twelve-year-old girl and
dumping her body in a pigsty. After more than ten years of
appeals and legal manoeuvring, a judge gave the order for
Bundy's execution. That week, he asked an attorney to call
me and request that I come to Florida State Prison for a final
interview.

When I arrived, I discovered a circus-like atmosphere
outside the prison. Teenagers carried signs saying, 'Burn,
Bundy Burn', and 'You're Dead, Ted'. Also in the crowd
were more than 300 reporters who had come to get a story
on the killer's last hours, but Bundy wouldn't talk to them.
He had something important to say, and he believed the
media couldn't be trusted to report it accurately. Therefore,
I was invited to bring a camera crew to record his last comments from death row.

I'll never forget that experience. I went through seven
steel doors and metal detectors so sensitive that my tie pin and the nails in my
shoes were enough to set off an alarm.
Finally, I reached an inner chamber
where Bundy and I were to meet. He
was brought in, strip-searched, and
then surrounded by six prison guards
while he talked to me. Midway through our conversation,
the lights suddenly went dim.

> *By the time he was apprehended, Bundy had killed at least twenty-eight young women and girls.*

Ted said, 'Just wait a moment, and they will come back on.'

I didn't realise until later what had happened. The prisoner knew that his executioners were testing the electric chair that would take his life the next morning.

TED BUNDY WANTED TO TELL
THE WORLD ABOUT PORNOGRAPHY

What was it that Ted Bundy was so anxious to say? He felt he owed it to society to warn of the dangers of hard-core pornography and to explain how it had led him to murder so many innocent women and girls. With tears in his eyes, he described the monster that took possession of him when he had been drinking. His craze to kill was always inflamed by violent pornography. Quoted below is an edited transcript of the conversation that occurred just seventeen hours before Ted was led to the electric chair. (Note: The seventh video in the *Life on the Edge* series, for which this book is a supplement, contains footage of the actual interview with Bundy and is available in bookstores or from Focus on the Family.)

DR DOBSON: Ted, it is about two-thirty in the afternoon. You are scheduled to be executed tomorrow morning at seven o'clock if you don't receive another stay. What is going through your mind? What thoughts have you had in these last few days?

TED BUNDY: Well, I won't kid you today that it's something that I feel that I'm in control of or something that I've come to terms with, because I haven't. It's a moment-by-moment thing.

DOBSON: Let's go back, then, to [your] roots. You, as I understand it, were raised in what you consider to have been a healthy home.

BUNDY: Absolutely.

DOBSON: You were not physically abused. You were not sexually abused. You were not emotionally abused.

BUNDY: No. No way. That's part of the tragedy of this whole situation, because I grew up in a wonderful home with two dedicated and loving parents. It was a fine, solid Christian home. But as a young boy—and I mean a boy of twelve or thirteen certainly—I encountered outside the home soft-core pornography. From time to time we'd come across pornographic books of a harder nature, more graphic you might say. And this also included such things as detective magazines . . .

DOBSON: And those that involved violence, then.

BUNDY: Yes, The most damaging kinds of pornography are those that involve sexual violence. Because the wedding of those two forces, as I know only too well, brings about behaviour that is just too terrible to describe.

DOBSON: Now I really want to understand that. You had gone about as far as you could go in your own fantasy life with printed material, and then there was the urge to take that little step or big step over to a physical event.

BUNDY: My experience with pornography that deals on a violent level with sexuality is that once you become addicted to it—and I look at this as a kind of addiction, like other kinds of addiction—I would keep looking for more potent, more explicit, more graphic kinds of material. Like an addiction, you keep craving something which is harder, harder. Something which gives you a greater sense of excitement. Until you reach the point where the pornography only goes so far. You reach that jumping-off point where you begin to wonder if maybe actually doing it will give you that which is beyond just reading about it or looking at it.

DOBSON: Do you remember what pushed you over that edge?

BUNDY: I knew that I couldn't control it anymore, that the barriers that I had learned as a child, that had been instilled in me, were not enough to hold me back with respect to seeking out and harming somebody.

DOBSON: Would it be accurate to call that a frenzy, a sexual frenzy?

BUNDY: Well, yes. That's one way to describe it. A compulsion, a building up of destructive energy. But I think that what alcohol did in conjunction with, let's say, my exposure to pornography [is that] alcohol reduced my inhibitions, at the same time. The fantasy life that was fuelled by pornography eroded them further, you see.

DOBSON: In the early days, you were nearly always about half-drunk when you did these things. Is that right?

BUNDY: Yes. Yes.

DOBSON: All right, if I can understand it now, there's this battle going on within. There are the conventions that you've been taught. And then there is this unbridled passion fuelled by your plunge into hard-core, violent pornography.

BUNDY: Well, yes. That is a major component, and I don't know why I was vulnerable to it. All I know is that it had an impact on me that was just so central to the development of the violent behaviour that I engaged in.

DOBSON: Ted, after you committed your first murder, what was the emotional effect on you? What happened in the days after that?

BUNDY: Again, please understand that even all these years later, it's very difficult to talk about it, and reliving it through talking about it. It was like coming out of some kind of horrible trance or dream. I can only liken it to, and I don't want to overdramatise it, but to have been possessed by something so awful and so alien, and then the next morning wake up from it, remember what happened, and realise that basically, you're responsible. To wake up in the morning and realise what I had done, with a clear mind and all my essential moral and ethical feelings intact at that moment, [I was] absolutely horrified that I was capable of doing something like that.

DOBSON: You really hadn't known that before?

BUNDY: I want people to understand this. Basically, I was a normal person. I wasn't some guy hanging out at bars, or a bum. Or I wasn't a pervert in the sense that people look at somebody and say, 'I know there's something wrong with him; I can just tell.' But I was essentially a normal person. I had good friends. I lived a normal life, except for this one small, but very potent, very destructive segment of it that I kept very secret, very close to myself, and didn't let anybody know about. And part of the shock and horror for my dear friends and family, years ago when I was first arrested, was that there was no clue. They looked at me, and they looked at the 'All-American' boy. I think people need to recognise that those of us who have been so much influenced by violence in the media—in particular pornographic violence— are not some kind of inherent monsters. We are your sons, and we are your husbands. And we grew up in regular families. And pornography can reach out and snatch a kid out of any house today. It snatched me out of my home twenty, thirty years ago, as diligent as my parents were, and they were diligent in protecting their children. And as good a Christian home as we had—and we had a wonderful Christian home—there is no protection against the kinds of influences that there are loose in a society that tolerates. [Bundy is in tears.]

DOBSON: Ted, outside these walls right now there are several hundred reporters that wanted to talk to you.

BUNDY: Yeah.

DOBSON: And you asked me to come here from California because you had something you wanted to say.

You really feel that hard-core pornography and the doorway to it, soft-core pornography, is doing untold damage to other people and causing other women to be abused and killed the way you did it.

BUNDY: Listen. I'm no social scientist, and I haven't done a survey. I mean, I don't pretend that I know what John Q. Citizen thinks about this. But I've lived in prison for a long time now. And I've met a lot of men who were motivated to commit violence just like me. And without exception, every one of them was deeply involved in pornography—without question, without exception—deeply influenced and consumed by an addiction to pornography. There's no question about it. The FBI's own study on serial homicide shows that the most common interest among serial killers is pornography.

DOBSON: That's true.

BUNDY: And it's real.

DOBSON: Ted, what would your life have been like without that influence? You can only speculate.

BUNDY: I'm absolutely certain [it] would not have involved this kind of violence that I have committed.

DOBSON: One of the most important questions as you come down to perhaps your final hours: Are you thinking about all those victims out there and their families who are so wounded?

BUNDY: Absolutely. I can only hope that those who I have harmed and those who I have caused so much grief— even if they don't believe my expression of sorrow and remorse—will believe what I'm saying now, that there is loose in their towns, in their communities, people like me today whose dangerous impulses are being fuelled day in and day out by violence in the media in its various forms, particularly sexual violence. And what scares me—and let's come into the present now because what I'm talking about happened twenty, thirty years ago, that is, in my formative stages. And what scares and appalls me, Dr Dobson, is when I see what's on cable TV, some of the films, some of the violence in the films that come into homes today was stuff that they wouldn't show in x-rated adult theatres thirty years ago.

DOBSON: The slasher films that you're talking about.

BUNDY: The stuff is—I'm telling you from personal experience—the most graphic violence on the screen. Particularly as it gets into the home to the children who may be unattended or unaware that they may be a Ted Bundy who has a vulnerability to this kind of behaviour, by that kind of film and that kind of violence.

DOBSON: Can you help me understand this desensitisation process that took place? What was going on in your mind?

BUNDY: Each time I harmed someone, each time I killed someone, there would be an enormous amount of horror, guilt, remorse afterwards. But then that impulse to do it again would come back even stronger. The unique thing about how this worked, Dr Dobson, is that I still felt, in my regular life, the full range of guilt and remorse about other things. Regret and . . .

DOBSON: You had this compartmentalised . . .

BUNDY: . . . compartmentalised, very well focused, very sharply focused area where it was like a black hole. It was like a crack. And everything that fell into that crack just disappeared. Does that make sense?

DOBSON: It does. One of the final murders that you committed, of course, was apparently little Kimberly Leach, twelve years of age. I think the public outcry is greater there because an innocent child was taken from a playground. What did you feel after that? Were there the normal emotions three days later? Where were you, Ted?

BUNDY: [Struggling for words] I can't really talk about that right now.

DOBSON: That's too painful.

BUNDY: I would like to convey to you what that experience is like, but I can't. I won't be able to talk about that . . . [continuing] I can't begin to understand—well, I can try, but I'm aware that I can't begin to understand the pain that the parents of these children—that I have, and these young women that I have harmed—feel. And I can't restore really much to them, if anything, and I won't pretend to. I don't even expect them to forgive me, and I'm not asking for it. That kind of forgiveness is of God. And if they have it, they have it, and if they don't, well, maybe they'll find it someday.

DOBSON: Do you deserve the punishment the state has inflicted upon you?

BUNDY: That's a very good question, and I'll answer it very honestly. I don't want to die. I deserve, certainly, the most extreme punishment society has, and I think society deserves to be protected from me and from others like me. That's the irony. What I'm talking about is going beyond retribution because there is no way in the world that killing me is going to restore those beautiful children to their parents and correct and soothe the pain. But I'll tell you, there are lots of other kids playing in streets around this country today who are going to be dead tomorrow and the next day and the next day and next month, because other young people are reading the kinds of things and seeing the kinds of things that are available in the media today.

DOBSON: And yet, you told me last night, and I have heard that you have accepted the forgiveness of Jesus Christ, and are a follower and a believer in Him. Do you draw strength from that as you approach these final hours?

BUNDY: I do. I can't say that being in the valley of the shadow of death is something that I've become all that accustomed to, and that I'm strong and nothing's bothering me. Listen, it's no fun. It gets kind of lonely, and yet, I have to remind myself that every one of us will go through this someday in one way or another . . . and countless millions who have walked this earth before us have, so this is just an experience which we all share. Here I am.

With that, Ted Bundy was led away with his arms cuffed behind his back. At seven o'clock the following morning, he was buckled into the electric chair, and his soul went into eternity. If anyone ever deserved to be executed, it was this man. He brutally killed without mercy and inflicted incredible pain on the families and friends of his victims. What a tragedy! There is a possibility, at least, that it would not have occurred if that thirteen-year-old boy had never stumbled upon pornographic magazines on a rubbish tip. He was one of those people who was terribly vulnerable to depictions of sexual violence.

Bundy was correct in saying that most serial murderers are addicted to hard-core pornography. FBI records validate that point. Not every person exposed to obscenity will become a killer, of course, but too many will! If only five or ten people in a nation become serial murderers per year, each killing twenty-eight people, it is too many!

Unfortunately, the willingness of men in our culture to harm women is far more widespread than that. Two researchers at UCLA studied this impulse among 'normal' university men. They asked hundreds of male students, 'Would you rape a woman if you knew you would never get caught?' More than fifty per cent said 'Yes'.

PORNOGRAPHY OFTEN LEADS
TO VIOLENT CRIME

Common sense tells us that providing potentially violent men with highly erotic depictions of rape, murder, and torture is dangerous and stupid. Yet there is very little restraint on what the pornographers are able to produce and sell in this country. And remember this: Hunters read hunting magazines, fishermen read fishing magazines, computer specialists read computer magazines, and you can be sure that men who find it exciting to assault women sexually read magazines and watch videos that depict that terrible abuse.

What does this discussion mean for you? Just this: Remember that pornography is dangerous. It can warp the mind and destroy sexual intimacy in marriage. Stay away from it. A monster is crouched behind this door.

In the next chapter, we'll walk on down the hallway to consider other forms of addictive behaviour.

12

FURTHER DOWN THE HALLWAY

Your generation has been the target of incredible disinformation on the subject of premarital sex, which is another enticing addictive behaviour to be considered. In this instance, our own government is responsible for much of the confusion. For the past twenty-one years, federal and state programmes have promoted a concept its promoters call 'safe sex', which refers to the use of condoms in sexual intercourse. More than three billion dollars have been spent telling young people that they can have sex—lots of really good sex—without suffering from the consequences of it.[1] Condoms, they say, will solve all the problems.

Well, how about it? How accurate is the information that has been taught in sex-education classes? What have we got for three billion dollars? And just how safe is 'safe sex'?

In a word, the great condom caper has been a social disaster. We are now facing an epidemic of sexually transmitted diseases (STDs) that is unprecedented. We hear every day about AIDS, which is only one of the terrible illnesses now afflicting the human family. But that is just the tip of the iceberg. More than twenty other STDs are running rampant throughout our society. Numerous bacterial infections that cause painful and dangerous symptoms are passing from person to person. One million cases of pelvic inflammatory disease occurs annually.[2] There are more cases of syphilis now than at any other time since the discovery of penicillin.[3] Gonorrhea is running wild, with 1.3 million new cases per year.[4] Four million cases of chlamydia are showing up annually.[5] And on it goes. In addition to bacterial STDs, most of which can be treated with antibiotics, there are numerous infections caused by viruses that cannot be cured. Indeed, the US. Centres for Disease Control calculated that fifty-six million people in the United States now have a sexually transmitted virus, and they will suffer from it for the rest of their lives.[6] Did that sink in? One in five Americans is infected with an incurable sexually transmitted virus! Among them is the disease known as herpes, which plagues an additional 500,000 people per year.[7]

STATISTICS TELL THE STORY

Not only do these illnesses cause pain and discomfort; many of them lead to infertility and other physical problems. Some actually kill their victims. Again, you've heard that HIV is deadly. But did you know that there is another virus of epidemic proportions that causes far more deaths among women than AIDS? Seven thousand American women die every year from the consequences of an organism called human papilloma virus (HPV).[8] It causes genital warts, and in some patients, leads to cancer of the cervix. In fact, it is estimated that ninety per cent of cervical cancer cases are caused by HPV, and the virus itself cannot be eradicated once it is in the system.[9]

Please read carefully: A medical investigation was conducted recently at the University of California at Berkeley. Averaging twenty-one years of age, all the young women coming to the campus health centre for routine gynaecological examinations were tested for HPV. Would you believe that forty-seven per cent of these students were found to carry this deadly virus? Every one of them will suffer painful symptoms for the rest of their lives, and some will die of cervical cancer.[10]

If I sound angry about what has happened to a generation of young people, you've read me right. These facts that I've shared, all of which are documented in respected medical journals, are being withheld from the public—especially from those of you in the critical decade. Sex educators seldom tell this story. They don't want you to hear it. Why? Because millions of dollars in federal grants are available to those who promote condom usage. There isnothing, or nearly nothing, available for the teaching of abstinence.

What about the use of condoms? How well do they work? If everyone practised 'safe sex' and never exposed themselves to 'unprotected intercourse', wouldn't the epidemic be solved? Good questions. Let's look at the facts.

THE TROUBLE WITH CONDOMS

Numerous medical studies have been conducted in recent years to evaluate the efficiency of condoms. Here are some of the findings: One important investigation showed that these latex devices fail 15.7 per cent of the time annually in preventing pregnancy.[11] Another said they fail 36 per cent of the time annually in preventing pregnancy among young, unmarried women.[12] Given these findings, it is obvious why we have a word for people who rely on condoms as a means of birth control. We call them 'parents'.

Remembering that a woman can conceive only a few days per month, we can only guess how much higher the failure rate for condoms must be in preventing disease, which can be transmitted 365 days per year! Those who would depend on so flimsy a method must use it properly on every occasion, and even then a high failure rate is brought about by factors beyond their control. If the devices slip or if they break or if they are defective or if they dry out in your wallet or purse, then viruses, bacteria, yeast, and fungi are exchanged, and disease processes begin. The damage is done in a single moment when rational thought is overridden by passion. One mistake after 500 'protected' episodes is all it takes to contract an STD. Lifelong pain, an unwanted pregnancy, and even death may be the reward for such a brief window of pleasure. What a foolish gamble!

There is another major problem with condoms. They do not cover the entire pubic region. Some diseases can be transmitted from the base of the penis or the testicles. So even if the device functions as intended and no mistakes are made during intercourse, disease can still be transmitted. I'll bet no one ever told you *that* in sex education classes!

What do medical researchers say about the ability of condoms to screen out viruses, which are much smaller than most bacteria? Well, for one thing, there is evidence that the human papilloma virus, described previously, can penetrate the latex rubber of a condom. That may account for the high rate of infection on university campuses.[13]

But how about the dreaded HIV? Does it get through the sheath, and if so, how often? That important question was evaluated at the University of Texas Medical Branch in Galveston. After reviewing eleven independent studies, the researchers concluded that condoms were only sixty-nine per cent effective in preventing the transmission of HIV. That may be reassuring to some, until you realise that a failure rate of thirty one per cent exposes huge numbers of users to HIV and eventual death from AIDS! Imagine picking up a gun having 100 chambers and thirty-one bullets. Would you put it to your head and pull the trigger? I certainly hope not. Nor would medical researchers. The doctor who led the investigation concluded, 'When it comes to the sexual transmission of HIV, the only real prevention is not to have sex with someone who has or might have HIV.' [14]

Perhaps this is why not one of 800 sexologists attending a conference raised a hand when asked if they would trust a thin rubber sheath to protect them during intercourse with a known HIV-infected person.[15] I don't blame them. They're not crazy, after all. Yet they're perfectly willing to tell your generation that 'safe sex' is within reach and you can sleep around with impunity. It is a terrible lie.

STDS: PANDEMIC IN PROPORTION

Speaking of 'sleeping around', it isn't necessary to have sex with numerous partners in order to contract an STD. If you are intimate with two or three people each year who are themselves having sex with a few others, you *will* become infected. That's one of the characteristics of an epidemic. If you expose yourself to it, you'll soon pick up the organisms that are going around. Maybe you'll be lucky and contract an STD that can be treated. But I wouldn't count on it. One in five Americans has already lost that gamble.[16]

One of the reasons STDs are so pandemic is that the micro-organisms that cause them remain on and in the reproductive organs almost indefinitely. The body does not cleanse itself of them. In fact, it has been said that when you have sex with someone, you are actually having sex with everyone who ever slept with that person. Unless specific treatment has eliminated the germs that have accumulated through the years, they are still there waiting for a new carrier to come along.

Well, that brings us to the point: There is only one way to protect ourselves from the deadly diseases that stalk the human family. It is abstinence before marriage, then marriage and mutual fidelity for life to an uninfected partner. Anything less is foolhardy and potentially suicidal. Don't let anyone tell you differently. There is no such thing as 'safe sex', just as there is no 'safe sin'. For thousands of years, people have been trying to find ways to disobey the laws of God without suffering the consequences. It can't be done. Scripture tells us that the wages of sin is death, and we'd better believe it!

What I am recommending to the unmarried person, therefore, comes straight out of the Word: Stay out of bed unless you go there alone! I know that advice is difficult to put into practise today. But I didn't make the rules. I'm just passing them along. God's moral laws are not designed to oppress us or deprive us of pleasure. They are there to protect us from the devastation of sin, including disease, heartache, divorce, and spiritual death. Abstinence before marriage and fidelity afterwards is the Creator's own plan, and no one has devised a way to improve on it.

LIFE-GIVING WISDOM FROM THE WORD

The wisest man who ever lived, King Solomon, wrote a letter to his son to warn him about the consequences of immorality. His words are recorded for us in Proverbs 6 and speak eloquently about the dangers of adultery. Listen to the passion of a father's heart:

My son, keep your father's commands
    and do not forsake your mother's teaching. . . .
When you walk, they will guide you;
    when you sleep, they will watch over you;
    when you awake, they will speak to you.
For these commands are a lamp,
    this teaching is a light,
and the corrections of discipline
    are the way to life,
keeping you from the immoral woman,
    from the smooth tongue of the wayward wife.
Do not lust in your heart after her beauty

or let her captivate you with her eyes,
for the prostitute reduces you to a loaf of bread,
 and the adulteress preys upon your very life.
Can a man scoop fire into his lap
 without his clothes being burned?
Can a man walk on hot coals
 without his feet being scorched?
So is he who sleeps with another man's wife;
 no one who touches her will go unpunished.

Proverbs 6:20, 22–29

The validity of Solomon's message has not changed in the 2,700 years since he penned it. It comes down through the corridors of time and echoes today with the authority of God Himself. Solomon tells us that the divine commandments are a 'light' that will show us 'the way to life'. But those who would disregard them, both male and female, will suffer the painful consequences.

FOREVER CLEANSED BY JESUS

Now I need to speak directly and with compassion to those who have already pushed open the door of premarital sex. The monster has been released. You've lost your virginity and may have been sexually active for years. Perhaps you've been carrying a load of guilt for doing what you knew was wrong. What do you do now? Is there any way back for you?

I'm delighted to tell you that Jesus Christ offers complete and total forgiveness to *anyone* who will repent and believe on His name. What a gift from His great heart! There are no sins that He cannot cleanse, and He's promised that they will be gone forever. He puts them in the sea of His forgetfulness, and hangs a 'No Fishing' sign on the bank. Let me give you a wonderful scripture you can hold on to when bad memories rise up before you:

> He will not always accuse,
>> nor will he harbour his anger forever;
> he does not treat us as our sins deserve
>> or repay us according to our iniquities.
> For as high as the heavens are above the earth,
>> so great is his love for those who fear him;
> as far as the east is from the west,
>> so far has he removed our transgressions from us.
>
> Psalms 103:9–12

Isn't that an incredible promise? The record of our sins can be banished to the other side of the universe. God Himself even 'forgets' the wickedness committed by those whom He has forgiven. That's why it is never too late to clean up your life.

Stay out of bed unless you go there alone!

Even if you have been having sex for years with many people, you can still become a 'secondary virgin'. That occurs when you repent of previous sexual sins and then determine not to be intimate with anyone until you are married. It will require discipline to stay in the hallway of doors, but it will bring the sweet benefits of healthiness, greater self-respect, and above all, harmony with the King. He will honour you for doing what is right.

Jesus Christ offers complete and total forgiveness.

Let's return, in conclusion, to the writings of Solomon. Remember that I have referred to a 'monster' that grabs and holds its victim. This is the way the wise old king described that danger for his son:

> For a man's ways are in full view of the Lord,
>> and he examines all his paths.
> The evil deeds of a wicked man ensnare him,
>> the cords of his sin hold him fast.
> He will die for lack of discipline,
>> led astray by his own great folly.　　Proverbs 5:21–23

There is a better way!

13

QUESTIONS FROM THE EDGE

I am nineteen years old, and I'm proud to say that I'm still a virgin. I plan to stay that way until I get married, even though it is difficult to control what I feel. Do you have any suggestions that will help people like me to be moral in a very immoral world? I mean, almost everyone I know is sleeping with somebody, and I don't want to do that. Still, I need help to do what is right. What do you suggest?

Well, I certainly admire your determination to save yourself for your future husband. You will never regret that decision. But in order to stick to it, you need to understand that sex is progressive in nature. The relationship between a guy and a girl naturally becomes more intimate as they spend time together.

In the early days they may be content to hold hands or have an occasional good-night kiss. But from that beginning, they typically become more physical week by week until they find themselves in bed. That's just the power of sex in our lives.

I read one study that indicated when a couple has been together for approximately 300 hours, even most of those who are trying to be moral will do things they didn't intend originally. They may not even realise that is where the relationship is headed until it happens.

What I'm saying is that the decision not to have sexual intercourse should be made long before the opportunity presents itself. Steps can then be taken to slow down the natural progression before it gets started. It doesn't work to allow all the preliminary intimacies and then hope to stop the progression just short of inter-course. Very few people have the will power to do that. Instead, a very early decision must be made to delay kissing, fondling, caressing, and other forms of phys-ical contact. Failure to put the relationship on a slower timetable may result in an act that was never intended in the first place.

Avoid the circumstances where compromise is likely.

Another important principle is to avoid the circum-stances where compromise is likely. A girl who wants to pre-serve her virginity should not find herself in a house or dorm room alone with someone to whom she is attracted. Nor should she single-date with someone she has reason not to trust. A guy who wants to be moral should stay away from the girl he knows would go to bed with him. Remember the words of Solomon to his son, 'Keep to a path far from her, do not go near her door or her house' (Pro-verbs 5:8).

I know this advice sounds very narrow in a day when vir-ginity is mocked and chastity is considered old-fashioned. But I don't apologise for it. The Scriptures are eternal, and God's standards of right and wrong do not change with the whims of culture. He will honour and help those who are trying to follow His commandments. In fact, the apostle Paul said, 'He will not let you be tempted beyond what you can bear (1 Corinthians 10:13). Hold that promise and con-tinue to use your head. You'll be glad you did.

the woman caught in the very act of intercourse—a capital offence in those days—than He was the hypocrites in the church. That is our model for how to respond to a person living in sin. Indeed, we should be trying to reach out to those who don't know Jesus Christ, which is impossible in an atmosphere of hostility.

Having said that, we are also obligated to take our values and our definition of right and wrong from the Scriptures. It doesn't matter what I think or what you think. The critical issue is what God thinks, and on this subject He has made Himself very clear. Let's look at the biblical references to homosexuality and lesbianism.

> If a man lies with a man as one lies with a woman, both of them have done what is detestable. (Leviticus 20:13)

> While they were enjoying themselves, some of the wicked men of the city surrounded the house. Pounding on the door, they shouted to the old man who owned the house, 'Bring out the man who came to your house so we can have sex with him.'

> The owner of the house went outside and said to them, 'No, my friends, don't be so vile.' (Judges 19:22–23)

> Because of this, God gave them over to shameful lusts. Even their women exchanged natural relations for unnatural ones. In the same way the men also abandoned natural relations with women and became inflamed with lust for one another. Men committed indecent acts with other men, and received in themselves the due penalty for their perversion. (Romans 1:26–27)

> Do you not know that the wicked will not inherit the kingdom of God? Do not be deceived: Neither the sexually immoral nor idolaters nor adulterers nor male prostitutes nor homosexual offenders nor thieves nor the greedy nor drunkards nor slanderers nor swindlers will inherit the kingdom of God. (1 Corinthians 6:9–10)

We know that the law is good if a man uses it properly. We also know that law is made not for good men but for law-breakers and rebels, the ungodly and sinful, the unholy and irreligious; for those who kill their fathers or mothers, for murderers, for adulterers and perverts, for slave traders and liars and perjurers—and for whatever else is contrary to the sound doctrine that confirms to the glorious gospel of the blessed God, which he entrusted to me. (1 Timothy 1:8–10)

Obviously, these scriptures leave little room for debate. The only way their message can be negated is to reject the authority of God's Word. But I would like to point out that many of those same texts and numerous others also condemn premarital heterosexuality with equal vigour. Immorality is immoral whether it occurs with people of the same sex or those of opposite sex. In both cases, our responsibility is to call sin by its name and to admonish men and women to live in purity and holiness.

> *Our responsibility is . . . to admonish men and women to live in purity and holiness.*

There is another aspect to this issue that needs to be clarified. Whereas we are obligated to treat gay and lesbian individuals with respect, we are morally responsible to oppose the radical agenda of the gay-rights movement. What they are trying to accomplish in our society is wrong, and it must be resisted.

That agenda includes teaching pro-homosexual concepts in state schools, redefining the family to represent 'any circle of people who love each other', approval of homosexual adoption, and special legal status for those who identify themselves as gay. I won't take the time to explain why each of these objectives is harmful, but we must resist them.

6. Do you think AIDS is God's plague sent to punish homosexuals, lesbians, and other promiscuous people?

I would think not, because babies and others who bear no responsibility are also suffering. But consider this: If I choose to leap off a ten-storey building, I will die when my body hits the ground. It's inevitable. But gravity was not designed by God to punish my folly. He established physical laws that can be violated only at great peril. So it is with His moral laws. They are as real and predictable as the principles that govern the physical universe.

Thus, we knew at the onset of the sexual revolution back in the late sixties that the day of disease and promiscuity would come. It is here, and what we do with our situation will determine how much we and our children will suffer in the future.

God created the moral basis for the universe before He made the heavens and the earth. His concept of right and wrong was not an afterthought that came along with the Ten Commandments. No, it was an expression of God's divine nature and was in force before 'the beginning'.

That's what we read in Proverbs 8:22–30, 32–36, referring to the universal moral law in first person:

> The Lord brought me forth as the first of his works,
>   before his deeds of old;
> I was appointed from eternity,
>   from the beginning, before the world began.
> When there were no oceans, I was given birth,
>   when there were no springs abounding with water;
> before the mountains were settled in place,
>   before the hills, I was given birth,
> before he made the earth or its fields
>   or any of the dust of the world.
> I was there when he set the heavens in place,
>   when he marked out the horizon on the face of the deep,
> when he established the clouds above
>   and fixed securely the fountains of the deep,

when he gave the sea its boundary
    so the waters would not overstep his command,
and when he marked out the foundations of the earth.
    Then I was the craftsman at his side.
I was filled with delight day after day,
    rejoicing always in his presence. . . .

Now then, my sons listen to me;
    blessed are those who keep my ways.
Listen to my instruction and be wise;
    do not ignore it.
Blessed is the man who listens to me,
    watching daily at my doors,
    waiting at my doorway.
For whoever finds me finds life
    and receives favour from the Lord
But whoever fails to find me harms himself;
    all who hate me love death.

That scripture is abundantly clear, and it applies equally to homosexual and heterosexual immorality. If we conform our behaviour to God's ancient moral prescription, we are entitled to the sweet benefits of life. But if we defy its imperatives, then death is the inevitable consequence. AIDS is only one avenue by which sickness and death befall those who play Russian roulette with God's eternal moral law.

7. Is homosexuality inherited, or is it an acquired trait?

There is controversy surrounding this question, primarily because gay-rights activists want people to believe that homosexuality is an involuntary, inherited characteristic. If the impulse towards gay and lesbianism are not chosen lifestyles, then those who participate in them are not responsible for the way they are. That position is not supportable by the facts, however, as I think I can show with this line of reasoning:

First, if homosexuality were specifically an inherited trait, then *all* identical twins would either have it or not have it. Their genes are exact duplicates, so anything deriving specifically from their genetic material would express itself identically in the two individuals. Such is not the case. There are thousands of identical twins in whom one is gay and the other is straight.

Second, inherited characteristics that are not passed on to the next generation are eliminated from the gene pool. Since homosexuals and lesbians experience parenthood less frequently than heterosexuals, there should be a decreasing number of people in the population with homosexual tendencies—especially over the many thousands of years mankind has been on the earth.

Third, Scripture refers to epidemics of homosexuality and lesbianism that have occurred in specific cultures. For example, Romans 1:26–27, quoted earlier, refers to such a time in ancient Rome:

> Because of this, God gave them over to shameful lusts. Even their women exchanged natural relations for unnatural ones. In the same way the men also abandoned natural relations with women and became inflamed with lust for one another. Men committed indecent acts with other men, and received in themselves the due penalty for their perversion.

That final sentence sounds like the transmission of sexually transmitted diseases, doesn't it?

Again, if homosexuality were inherited within the human family, it would be a constant over time. There would not be surges and epidemics as the apostle Paul referred to and as we are seeing today.

Fourth, God is infinitely reasonable and just. I don't

believe He would speak of homosexuality in the Scripture as an abominable sin and list it among the most despicable human behaviours if men and women bore no responsibility for engaging in it. That is not how He does business.

While homosexuality and lesbianism are not genetically induced characteristics, it is accurate to say that it often occurs in those who did not choose it. Children who were

> *God is infinitely reasonable and just.*

sexually abused as children, those coming from troubled homes, and those experiencing other kinds of trauma may be predisposed to gay lifestyles. Others are drawn towards the gay lifestyle in the absence of any known related influences. Such individuals need our care and compassion as they struggle to deal with the forces that lie within. We can accept them without approving of behaviour the Bible condemns.

8. So what does God expect of a person who is homosexual but who wants to live a Christian life?

Well, there is no sin in *being* gay. The immorality comes from engaging in forbidden behaviour. Therefore, the Christian homosexual is in the same situation as the unmarried heterosexual. They are expected to control their lusts and live a holy life. I know this is a tough position to take, and some will argue with it. But I stand on the authority of Scripture, and I have no licence to edit it.

9. What do you think about 'date rape' when a girl has given a guy the come on? If she has flirted with him and gone with him to an apartment or to someplace she shouldn't be, doesn't he have the right to have sex with her?

A guy *never* has a right to force a woman to have sex with

him under any circumstances. She should be able to say no at any point, and he must honour that denial. It is criminal that so many girls and women are raped today. Fully sixty per cent of all females who lose their virginity before the age of fifteen say that their first sexual experience was forced![4] This is a tragedy with far-reaching consequences.

What concerns me is that society has taught young men that they have the right to force themselves on young women. In a study conducted by the Rhode Island Rape Crisis Centre, 1,700 students between the sixth and ninth grades were asked if a man should have a right to force a woman to have sexual intercourse with him under certain circumstances. Sixty-five per cent of the boys and forty-seven per cent of the girls said boys do have that right if they have dated a girl for six months or longer! And fifty-one per cent of the boys said a guy has a right to force a girl to kiss him if he spent 'a lot of money on her'—defined by twelve-year-olds as ten to fifteen dollars.[5]

No wonder women find themselves on the defensive so often today. Men fully expect them to prostitute themselves if they've spent a few bucks on them.

Let me leave you with this thought written by my father before he died. If you incorporate it into your system of values, it will serve as a worthy guide to the management of your sexual energy:

> Strong desire is like a river. As long as it flows within the banks of God's will—be the current strong or weak—all is well. But when it overruns those boundaries and seeks its own channels, then disaster lurks in the rampage below.

14

CHOOSING A COLLEGE

Let's change gear now and talk about another very practical issue. Since some of my readers are in the younger years of the critical decade, I will devote this chapter to a question that they (you) may be considering. It is this: 'Where should I go to college?'

Not everyone plans to go into higher education, of course, and that's OK. We don't all have to fit in the same mould. But for those who do intend to continue their training, I want to offer a few thoughts that may be helpful.

First, I need to admit that I am not unbiased in the advice I'm about to offer. I'm going to give you one man's opinion that may differ from what you'll hear from your parents, your school counsellor, or your pastor. At least you know I've laid the cards on the table and confessed my lack of objectivity on this matter.

The issue at hand concerns whether to attend a Christian college or a state-sponsored (secular) college or university. In that debate, I believe strongly in Christian education for those of you who are followers of Christ. My wife and I are products of a church-sponsored college that made an incredible contribution to our lives. Both our children graduated from Christian universities, and we're delighted that they did. I will explain why in a moment.

Let me acknowledge that many students thrive academically and spiritually in large, secular schools, and they do not regret their decision to go there. Some get involved in Christian ministries on campus and emerge with their faith intact. Furthermore, there are thousands of dedicated Christian professors in public universities, and they believe God has led them to teach in that environment. In no way do I challenge that assumption or intend any disrespect whatsoever.

THE CASE AGAINST STATE UNIVERSITIES

Nevertheless, I am very concerned about some of the disturbing trends in state or secular schools, and you should know what you will experience if you choose to attend one of them. Frankly, I would not send my son or daughter there under normal circumstances, for the following reasons:

1. Secular universities today are bastions of moral relativism that leave no room for the Christian world-view.

I doubt if many students or their parents realise just how antagonistic many of our state schools have become to anything that smacks of Christianity. There is simply no place for God in the system. The new god is 'diversity', which respects all world-views and philosophies—except one. The Christian perspective is not only excluded from the classroom, it is often ridiculed and undermined.

I am very concerned about some of the disturbing trends in public or secular schools.

The dominant philosophy in today's state university is called relativism, which categorically denies the existence of truth or moral absolutes. Those who are foolish enough to believe in such archaic notions as biblical authority or the claims of Christ are to be pitied—or bullied.

That is the prevailing attitude in most state-sponsored institutions today.

2. State universities are dominated by 'politically correct' (PC) thought that can be contradicted only at great personal sacrifice.

There is, perhaps, less freedom of thought on today's secular campuses than any other place in society. A student or faculty member is simply not permitted to espouse ideas that are contrary to the approved 'group think'. This purity is enforced by what has been called 'campus thought police', including feminist extremists on the faculty, homosexual and lesbian activists, leftist professors, minority activists, and bilingual advocates. Donald Kagan, former dean of Yale College, said, 'I was a student during the days of Joseph McCarthy, and there is less freedom now than there was then.' [1]

According to Todd Ackerman, writing in *The Houston Chronicle,* at least 250 universities now have 'speech codes' to which students must conform.[2] What are some of the ideas that they censor? John Leo, writing in *US News and World Report,* listed these forbidden topics: 'the SAT, doubt about abortion, Catholics, wearing fur, any emphasis on standards of excellence, and any suggestion that gender and ethnicity might not be the most overwhelmingly important issues of the modern era.' [3]

Here are a few examples of political correctness in action:

* Pennsylvania State University advised its 10,000

incoming freshmen in 1990 that they might be assigned a homosexual room-mate, and if so, they would not be permitted to object.[4]

* At New York University Law School, students refused to debate a mock court case involving a hypothetical divorced lesbian mother trying to win custody of her child because arguing against would be hurtful to gays.[5]

* At Harvard University, a leading liberal historian of race relations, Stephen Thernstrom, was vilified as a 'racist' for endorsing Senator Patrick Moynihan's views on the social ills caused by the collapse of the black family and using such terms as 'American Indian' instead of 'Native American'.[6]

* The University of Michigan has established a 'student guide to proper behaviour' that indiscriminately lumps racist threats with such conduct as 'failing to invite someone to a party because she's a lesbian'.[7]

* While Secretary of Health and Human Services Donna Shalala was chancellor of the University of Wisconsin-Madison, its board of regents implemented a written policy requiring politically correct speech. The document was so extreme it was declared unconstitutional by a federal court.[8]

3. The politically correct philosophy on many campuses disdains Western civilisation, with its emphasis on the Judeo/Christian heritage.

Many of the more prestigious universities, including Stanford, have eliminated their 'core curriculum' based on Western civilisation. It is, they say, inherently unfair to minorities, women, and homosexuals. Great disrespect is expressed on these campuses for the literature, science, art, religious heritage, and history of European forefathers (pardon *Me!* fore*people*!). Much less emphasis is given to the study of Shakespeare, Mozart, Newton, Galileo, the British monarchy, and the significant events in European history. In fact, it is possible to graduate from seventy-eight per cent of America's colleges and universities without taking a course in Western civilisation.[9]

The consequence? Lynne Cheney, former chairman of the National Endowment for the Humanities, wrote that many students earn Bachelor degrees without knowledge of 'basic landmarks of history and thought'.[10] For example, in a 1989 Gallup poll, twenty-five per cent of 700 college seniors did not know that Columbus landed in the Western Hemisphere before 1500. Most could not identify the Magna Carta.[11] In short, what has constituted a liberal arts education for the past 200 years is undergoing a radical transformation. The revolution began by eliminating the concept of truth, and from there it dumped the common heritage that has bound us together as a people. Diversity, rather than cohesiveness, is the new passion, and it pits us against each other for 'rights'.

4. State universities are breeding grounds, quite literally, for sexually transmitted diseases (including HIV), homosexual behaviour, unwanted pregnancies, abortions, alcoholism, and drug abuse.

As public universities exercise tighter and tighter control on politically correct thought, they seem entirely disinterested in student sexual activity and other behaviour with moral implications. Indeed, the

> *Diversity, rather than cohesiveness, is the new passion.*

word *morality* itself implies a value judgement that violates PC 'theology'.

For example, administrators at the University of California at Berkeley were paralysed for months over what to do about the behaviour of 'the naked guy'. In the autumn of 1992, a student named Andrew Martinez made a practise of walking around the campus in the nude. He jogged, ate in the dining halls, and attended classes while totally naked. When asked why he wore no clothes, he said he was protesting sexually repressive traditions in Western society. Female students were uncomfortable in his presence, and both males and females were nervous about the 'seat issue'—not wanting to sit where he had recently sat.

It is unbelievable that it took the administrators all autumn and winter to deal with this outrage. They couldn't come up with a legal excuse or a school regulation that would require 'the naked guy' to either get dressed or get lost. Instead, every precaution was taken not to violate his rights. Remember, many administrators have no difficulty in expelling a student who utters an unwelcome opinion about the immorality of homosexuality.

At one point, Martinez was expelled under a hastily written policy banning public nudity, but he was immediately invited back when school officials realised they had not obtained a vice chancellor's approval for the decision. What a graphic illustration of the moral confusion of our day. Finally in late January, Martinez was sent packing. How did they finally get him out? Some female students charged that his behaviour constituted 'sexual harassment'! That says it all, doesn't it? The man was not expelled for violating established standards of decency. He had to trip over a tenet of political correctness before he could be thrown out on his naked rear end.

I understand Mr Martinez is now preparing a lawsuit against the university. That figures. Hard-pressed Californians paid taxes to give this ungrateful 'dude' an education, and he threw it in their faces. Then the administrators at Cal. Berkeley pathetically allowed him to mock the entire system! [12]

As for sexual behaviour on other campuses, consider these illustrations:

* Cornell University's Student Assembly recently recommended that a dormitory wing be reserved for about sixty students interested in promoting 'gay, lesbian and bisexual awareness'. [13]

* Since last autumn, about twenty students at the University of Massachusetts at Amherst have lived in a gay-lesbian-bisexual 'corridor'. The University of California has about forty students living in two gay 'theme' dormitories, and Rutgers University started a gay studies living unit for about ten students a few years ago. The idea is spreading.

* A study at a University of Texas student health centre revealed that nearly one in a hundred students seeking medical care is infected with the virus that causes AIDS. [15]

* Seventy-five per cent of students visiting the Cowell Health Centre at Stanford University describe themselves as 'sexually active'. [16]

These are only a few of my concerns about the state university system as it is currently operated. It is sad to realise that our most intelligent and promising students must face relativistic philosophies that would have horrified past generations. If you choose to continue your education in one of these institutions, at least you will know what to expect when you get there.

THE CASE FOR CHRISTIAN COLLEGES

But what about the colleges and universities that represent themselves as 'Christian'? Have they avoided all the pitfalls and immorality described previously? Some have not, but most are a breed apart. I thank God for schools that are serious about the gospel of Jesus Christ. They are vital to perpetuating our faith through your generation and beyond.

Here are a few of the reasons I believe so strongly in Christian education:

1. It is difficult to overestimate the importance of having godly professors for students in their late teens and early twenties.

My great concern for those of you in the young-adult years is that you are extremely vulnerable to the leadership of your professors. One of the primary reasons education changes people is that students admire and identify with those who tower over them in experience, training, maturity, intelligence, and charisma. This makes a young man or woman an easy mark for older adults who want to reorder their basic beliefs and value systems.

> *I thank God for schools that are serious about the gospel of Jesus Christ.*

Anyone who holds the power to fail a student finds it easy to prevail in debates about faith, morals, or philosophy! That's why we must continue to support godly men and women who have dedicated their lives to Christian principles and to continuing those ideas in our offspring. Professors' world-views influence whatever they teach, from the humanities to the basic sciences, and what they think about God cannot be hidden from their students.

2. Christian education places its emphasis on 'unity' in relationships between people.

As we have indicated, secular institutions have become almost obsessed with the concept of diversity in university life. What this means in practical terms is that people become fractionalised into competing self-interest groups. African-Americans are pitted against Hispanics who are at war with Asians who resent Native Americans who must compete with homosexuals and lesbians for status and territory. At an Academy Awards event a few years ago, for example, the emphasis on 'women in entertainment' was a prime case in point. It is impossible to credit one gender with every good and perfect gift without slighting the other. That's what extreme diversity does to us. Indeed, a recent issue of *Newsweek* featured the last American group to be victimised—white males.[17] Now we *all* have something to fight for.

> *Having no common values, heritage, commitment, or hope, . . . we are a nation in serious trouble.*

Abraham Lincoln quoted the Scriptures in an 1858 speech to the Illinois Republican Convention. He said, 'A house divided against itself cannot stand'.[18] That, I fear, is where diversity leads. If by that term we refer to love and tolerance for peoples who are different from one another, it has great validity for us. But if by *diversity* we mean all of us have been given reason to resent one another, having no common values, heritage, commitment, or hope, then we are a nation in serious trouble.

Whether right or wrong, it is *my* belief that Christian colleges place their emphasis not on that which divides us, but on the substance that binds us together. That commonality is the gospel of Jesus Christ. He commanded us to love one another—to set aside our differences and to care for 'the least of these' among us. It is our unity, not our diversity, that deserves our allegiance.

Though Christian professors and administrators have not always succeeded in this effort, unity has been (and continues to be) the goal. In short, they seek to bring their students and faculty together rather than dividing them into competing self-interest groups. I think that is a vitally important distinction.

3. I firmly believe students typically get a better undergraduate education at a Christian institution than at a large public institution.

State universities have earned most of their reputations for excellence from the quality of the research conducted in their graduate schools. Much less attention is given to teaching undergraduates. Professors are rewarded and promoted for their scientific findings and the number of publications they produce. Their ability to inspire and teach is of little consequence in advancement. Thus, freshmen and second year students often find themselves in huge classes of 300 to 2,000.

The instructor may be an inexperienced graduate student whose primary interest is their own academic pursuit. I know this system very well. I taught such a class at USC when I was working on my Ph.D.

The situation on Christian campuses is usually very different. Students often develop close relationships with their professors. The classes are usually smaller, permitting interaction and more opportunity to ask questions. Informal discussions at the professor's home or in a restaurant are not unusual. When compared to the education of perhaps 30,000 students at a state university, there is no doubt in my mind as to where the best training for undergraduates occurs.

4. A Christian college is the only place where the majority of students are professing Christians. That is vitally important.

The single greatest influence during the college years does not come from the faculty. It is derived from other students! Thus, being classmates with men and women who profess a faith in Jesus Christ is vital to the bonding that should occur during these years.

In addition to formal learning in the classroom, a quality education involves a wide variety of experiences with friends who share basic values and beliefs. These include dorm parties, chapel programmes, internal school and intercollegiate athletics, debates and seminars, a range of musical and dramatic groups, dorm Bible-study groups, and evenings in faculty member homes.

The friendships that flow from these activities will be remembered for a lifetime. Likewise, if it is important to marry someone who shares your Christian faith (and I think that is extremely important), then it seems wise to select a college where more Christians will be found.

The students Shirley and I met while attending a Christian college are still among our best friends today—more than thirty years later. There are no friends quite like those made during your younger years, and not one of them can be replaced in later life. I thank God for the experiences we had among guys and girls of like mind, faith, and values when we were very young!

I know that many families feel they can't afford a high-quality Christian college for their son or daughter. That may be the barrier in your family. Actually, I have found that Christian schools often charge less than comparable secular institutions. But I know that doesn't solve the problem.

You should know that most Christian colleges are

accustomed to serving low-income families or those where parents have lost their jobs or experienced long-term sickness. You would be amazed to hear how God has provided for their needs through financial aid, federal grants and loans, work programmes, and special student scholarships.

Before you rule out a private education, therefore, I hope you'll check the possibilities. I also recommend that you do not plan to attend a community college for the first two years unless it's absolutely necessary. The freshman and second years are the most important in terms of personal growth and development.

If you are thinking about attending a Christian college and don't know how to find the right one, you can buy an inexpensive handbook in Christian bookshops. It's called *Choose a Christian College,* released by Peterson's Guides, one of the largest publishers of college handbooks. While not covering every Christian College in North America, this volume includes information on eighty-four member colleges and universities of the Christian College Coalition. Each of these schools meets eight membership criteria, including a commitment by the administration to hiring as full-time faculty only people with a personal commitment to Jesus Christ. *Choose a Christian College* also provides information on tuition costs, grants and aid, available majors, entrance requirements, and campus life factors.

> *Christian schools often charge less than comparable secular institutions.*

I hope this discussion has been helpful in clarifying your own views on higher education. Now I suggest you seek advice and counsel from others you trust.

15

WHEN GOD DOESN'T MAKE SENSE

I want to turn our attention now to a concept that will help you remain steady when hardships and stresses challenge you as you live life on the edge. The following discussion from my book *When God Doesn't Make Sense* deals with our inability to explain everything He is doing in our lives, especially when the storm clouds gather. Let me begin with a few illustrations of this kind of confusion.

Chuck Frye was a bright young man of seventeen, academically gifted and highly motivated. After graduating near the top of his class in high school, he went on to college where he continued to excel in his studies. Upon completion of his Bachelor of Science degree, he applied for admittance to several medical schools.

The competition for acceptance in medical school was, and is, fierce. At the time, I was a professor at the University of Southern California School of Medicine, where only 106 students were admitted each year out of 6,000 applicants. That was typical of accredited medical programmes in that era. Despite these long odds, Chuck was accepted at the University of Arizona School of Medicine, and began his formal training.

During that first term, Chuck was thinking about the call of God on his life. He began to feel that he should forego high-tech medicine in some lucrative setting in favour of service on a foreign field. This eventually became his definite plan for the future. Towards the end of that first year of training, however, Chuck was not feeling well. He began experiencing a strange and persistent fatigue. He made an appointment for an examination in May and was soon diagnosed with acute leukemia. By November Chuck Frye was dead.

How could Chuck's heartbroken parents then, and how can we now, make sense of this incomprehensible act of God? This young man loved Jesus Christ with all his heart and sought only to do His will. Why was he taken in his prime despite many agonised prayers for his healing by godly family members and faithful friends? The Lord clearly said 'No' to them all. But why?

> *The Lord clearly said 'No' to them all. But why?*

Thousands of young doctors complete their education every year and enter the medical profession, some for less-than-admirable reasons. A tiny minority plan to spend their professional lives with the down-and-outs of the world. But here was a marvellous exception. If permitted to live, Chuck could have treated thousands of poor and needy people who otherwise would have suffered and died in utter hopelessness. Not only could he have ministered to their physical needs, but his ultimate desire was to share the gospel with those who had never heard this greatest of stories. Thus, his death simply made no sense.

Visualise with me the many desperately ill people Dr Chuck Frye might have touched in his lifetime, some with cancer, some with tuberculosis, some with congenital disorders, and some being children too young to even understand their pain. Why would divine Providence deny them his dedicated service?

There is another dimension to the Frye story that completes the picture. Chuck became engaged to be married in March of that first year in medical school. His fianceé was Karen Ernst, who was also a committed believer in Jesus Christ. She learned of Chuck's terminal illness six weeks after their engagement, but she chose to go through with their wedding plans.

They became husband and wife less than four months before his tragic death. Karen then enrolled in medical school at the University of Arizona, and after graduation, became a medical missionary in Swaziland, South Africa. Dr Karen Frye served there in a church-sponsored hospital until 1992. I'm sure she wonders—amidst so much suffering—why her brilliant young husband was not allowed to fulfil his mission as her medical colleague. And yes, I wonder, too.

> *God's purpose in this young man's demise is a mystery, and there it must remain.*

The great theologians of the world can contemplate the dilemma posed by Chuck Frye's death for the next fifty years, but they are not likely to produce a satisfying explanation. God's purpose in this young man's demise is a mystery, and there it must remain. Why, after much prayer, was Chuck granted admittance to medical school if he could not live to complete his training? From whence came the missions call to which he responded?

Why was so much talent invested in a young man who would not be able to use it? And why was life abbreviated in such a mature and promising student, while many drug addicts, winos, and evil-doers survive into old age as burdens on society? These troubling questions are much easier to pose than to answer. And . . . there are many others.

ALL WE CAN ASK IS 'WHY?'

The Lord has not yet revealed His reasons for permitting the plane crash that took the lives of my four friends in 1987. They were among the finest Christian gentlemen I have ever known. Hugo Schoellkopf was an entrepreneur and an extremely able member of the board of directors for Focus on the Family. George Clark was a bank president and a giant of a man. Dr Trevor Mabrey was a gifted surgeon who performed nearly half of his operations at no charge to his patients. He was a soft touch for anyone with a financial need. And Creath Davis was a minister and author who was loved by thousands. They were close friends who met regularly to study the Word and assure mutual accountability for what they were learning. I loved these four men. I had been with them the night before that last flight, when their twin-engine plane went down in the Absaroka mountain range in Wyoming. There were no survivors. Now, their precious wives and children are left to struggle on alone.

Why? What purpose was served by their tragic loss? Why are Hugo and Gail's two sons, the youngest of the children among the four families, deprived of the influence of their wise and compassionate father during their formative years? I don't know, although the Lord has given Gail sufficient wisdom and strength to carry on alone.

At the first mention of the 'awesome why', I think also of our respected friends, Jerry and Mary White. Dr White is president of the Navigators, a worldwide organisation dedicated to knowing Christ and making Him known. The Whites are wonderful people who love the Lord and live by the dictates of Scripture. But they have already had their share of suffering. Their son Steve drove a taxi for several months while seeking a career in broadcasting. But he would never achieve his dream. Steve was murdered by a deranged passenger late one night in the usually quiet city of Colorado Springs.

The killer was a known villain and drug abuser who had history of criminal activity. When he was appre-hended, the police learned that he had called for the cab with the intention of shooting whoever arrived to pick him up. Any number of drivers might have responded. Steve White took the call. It was random brutality beyond any rhyme or reason. And it occurred within a family that had honoured and served God for years in full-time Christian service.

Further examples of inexplicable sorrows and difficulties could fill the shelves of the world's largest library, and every person on earth could contribute illustrations of their own. Wars, famines, diseases, natural disasters, and untimely deaths are never easy to rationalise. But large-scale miseries of this nature are sometimes less troubling to the individual than the circumstances that confront each of us personally. Cancer, kidney failure, heart disease, sudden infant death syndrome, cerebral palsy, Down's syndrome, divorce, rape, loneliness, rejection, failure, infertility, widowhood— these and a million other sources of human suffering produce inevitable questions that trouble the soul. Why would God permit this to happen to me!? It is a question every believer—and many Pagans—have struggled to answer. And contrary to Christian teachings in some circles, the Lord typically does not rush in to explain what He is doing.

> *Examples of inexplicable sorrows and difficulties could fill the shelves of the world's largest library.*

THE SOVEREIGNTY OF GOD

If you believe God is obligated to explain Himself to us, you ought to examine the Scripture. Solomon wrote in Proverbs 25:2, 'It is the glory of God to conceal a matter. . . .' Isaiah 45:15 states, 'Truly you are a God who hides himself'. First Corinthians 2:11 says, '. . . No one knows the thoughts of God except the Spirit of God'. Deuteronomy 29:29 reads, 'The secret things belong to the Lord our God' (NKJV). Ecclesiastes 11:5 proclaims, 'As you do not know the path of the wind, or how the body is formed in a mother's womb, so you cannot understand the work of God, the Maker of all things.' Isaiah 55:8–9 teaches, ' "For my thoughts are not your thoughts, neither are your ways my ways,' declares the Lord. 'As the heavens are higher than the earth, so are my ways higher than your ways and my thoughts than your thoughts." '

Clearly, Scripture tells us we lack the capacity to grasp God's infinite mind or the way He intervenes in our lives. How arrogant of us to think otherwise. Trying to analyse His omnipotence is like an amoeba attempting to comprehend the behaviour of man. Romans 11:33 (NKJV) indicates that God's judgements are 'unsearchable' and His ways 'past finding out!' Similar language is found in 1 Corinthians 2:16: 'Who has known the mind of the Lord that he may instruct him?' Clearly, unless the Lord chooses to explain Himself to us, which He does not often do, His motivation and purposes are beyond the reach of mortal man.

What this means in practical terms is that many of our questions—especially those that begin with the word 'why'—will have to remain unanswered for the time being.

The apostle Paul referred to the problem of unanswered questions when he wrote, 'Now we see but a poor reflection as in a mirror; then we shall see face to face. Now I know in part; then I shall know fully, even as I am fully known' (1 Corinthians 13:12). Paul was explaining that we will not have the total picture until we meet in eternity, and by implication, we must learn to accept that partial understanding.

GOD'S WONDERFUL PLAN?

Unfortunately, many young believers—and some older ones, too—do not know that there will be times in every person's life when circumstances don't add up—when God doesn't appear to make sense. This aspect of the Christian faith is not well advertised. We tend to teach new Christians the portions of our theology that are attractive to a secular mind. For example, Campus Crusade for Christ (an evangelistic ministry I respect highly) has distributed millions of booklets called *The Four Spiritual Laws.* The first of these scriptural principles states, 'God loves you and offers a wonderful plan for your life.' That statement is certainly true. However, it implies that a believer will always comprehend the 'wonderful plan' and that they will approve of it. That may not be true.

For some people, such as Joni Eareckson Tada, the 'wonderful plan' means life in a wheelchair as a quadriplegic. For others it means early death, poverty, or the scorn of society. For the prophet Jeremiah, it meant being cast into a dark dungeon. For other Bible characters it meant execution. Even in the most terrible of circumstances, however, God's plan is 'wonderful' because anything in harmony with His will ultimately '. . . works for the good of those who love him, who have been called according to his purpose' (Romans 8:28).

> *There will be times in every person's life when circumstances don't add up.*

Still, it is not difficult to understand how confusion can develop at this point, especially for those of you who are young. During the springtime of your years, when health is good and the hardships, failures, and sorrows have not yet blown through your tranquil world, it is relatively easy to fit the pieces in place. You can honestly believe, with good evidence, that it will always be so. At that point, however, you are extremely vulnerable to spiritual confusion.

Dr Richard Selzer is a surgeon and a favourite author of mine. He writes the most beautiful and compassionate descriptions of his patients and the human dramas they confront. In his book *Letters to a Young Doctor*, he said that most young people seem to be protected for a time by an imaginary membrane that shields them from horror. They walk in it every day but are hardly aware of its presence.

As the immune system protects the human body from the unseen threat of harmful bacteria, so this mythical membrane guards them from life-threatening situations. Not every young person has this protection, of course, because children do die of cancer, congenital heart problems, and other disorders. But most of them are shielded—and don't realise it. Then, as the years roll by, one day it happens. Without warning, the membrane tears, and horror seeps into a person's life or into the life of a loved one. It is at this moment that an unexpected theological crisis presents itself.

NO GREATER LOVE

So what am I suggesting—that our heavenly Father is uncaring or unconcerned about His vulnerable sons and daughters, that He taunts us mere mortals as some sort of cruel, cosmic joke? It is almost blasphemous to write such nonsense. Every description given to us in Scripture depicts God as infinitely loving and kind, watching over His earthly children tenderly and guiding the

> *Every description given to us in Scripture depicts God as infinitely loving and kind.*

steps of the faithful. He speaks of us as 'his people, the sheep of his pasture' (Psalm 100:3). This great love led Him to send His only begotten Son as a sacrifice for our sin that we might escape the punishment we deserve. He did this because He 'so loved the world' (John 3:16).

The apostle Paul expressed it this way: 'For I am convinced that neither death nor life, neither angels nor demons, neither the present nor the future, nor any powers, neither height nor depth, nor anything else in all creation, will be able to separate us from the love of God that is in Christ Jesus our Lord' (Romans 8:38–39). Isaiah conveyed this message to us directly from the heart of the Father: 'So do not fear, for I am with you; do not be dismayed, for I am your God. I will strengthen you and help you; I will uphold you with my righteous right hand' (Isaiah 41:10). No, the problem here is not with the love and mercy of God.

One of the most breathtaking concepts in all of Scripture is the revelation that God knows each of us personally and that we are in His mind both day and night. There is simply no way to comprehend the full implications of this love by the King of kings and Lord of lords. He is all-powerful and all-knowing, majestic and holy, from everlasting to everlasting. Why would He care about us—about our needs, our welfare, our fears? We have been discussing situations in which God doesn't make sense. His concern for us mere mortals is the most inexplicable of all.

Job also had difficulty understanding why the Creator would be interested in human beings. He asked, 'What is man that you make so much of him, that you give him so much attention, that you examine him every morning?' (Job 7:17–18). David contemplated the same question when he wrote, 'What is man that you are mindful of him, the son of man that you care for him?' (Psalm 8:4). And again in Psalm 139, we read, 'O Lord, you have searched me and you know

me. You know when I sit and when I rise; you perceive my
thoughts from afar. You discern my going out and my lying

*'As a father has
compassion on
his children, so
the Lord has
compassion on
those who fear
him.'
—Psalm 103:13*

down; you are familiar with all my
ways. Before a word is on my tongue
you know it completely, O Lord' (vv.
1–4). What an incredible concept!

Not only is the Lord 'mindful' of
each one of us, but He describes
Himself throughout Scripture as our
Father. In Luke 11:13 we read, 'If you
then, though you are evil, know how

to give good gifts to your children, how much more will
your Father in heaven give the Holy Spirit to those who ask
him!' Psalm 103:13 says, 'As a father has compassion on his
children, so the Lord has compassion on those who fear
him.' But on the other hand, He is likened to a mother in
Isaiah 66:13: 'As a mother comforts her child, so will I comfort you.'

A FATHER'S LOVE

Being a parent of two children, both now grown, I can identify with these parental analogies. They help me begin to
comprehend how God feels about us. If necessary, Shirley
and I would give our lives for Danae and Ryan in a heartbeat. We pray for them every day, and they are never very far
from our thoughts. And how vulnerable we are to their
pain! Can it be that God actually loves His human family
infinitely more than we, 'being evil', can express to our own
flesh and blood? That's what the Word teaches.

An incident occurred during our son's early childhood
that illustrated for me this profound love of the heavenly
Father. Ryan had a terrible ear infection when he was three
years old that kept him (and us) awake most of the night.

Shirley bundled up our toddler the next morning and took him to see the paediatrician. This doctor was an elderly man with very little patience for squirming kids. He wasn't overly fond of parents, either.

After examining Ryan, the doctor told Shirley that the infection had adhered itself to the eardrum and could only be treated by pulling the scab loose with a wicked little instrument. He warned that the procedure would hurt and instructed Shirley to hold him tightly on the table. Not only did this news alarm her, but enough of it was understood by Ryan to send him into orbit. (It didn't take much to do that in those days.)

Shirley did the best she could. She put Ryan on the examining table and attempted to hold him down. But he would have none of it. When the doctor inserted the pick-like instrument in his ear, the child broke loose and screamed to high heaven. The paediatrician then became angry at Shirley and told her if she couldn't follow instructions she'd have to get her husband. I was in the neighbourhood and quickly came to the examination room. After hearing what was needed, I swallowed hard and wrapped my 200-pound, six-foot-two-inch frame around our son. It was one of the toughest moments in my career as a parent.

What made it so emotional was the long mirror Ryan was facing as he lay on the examining table. This made it possible for him to look directly at me as he screamed for mercy. I really believed I was in greater agony at that moment than my terrified little boy. It was too much. I turned him loose—and got a beefed-up version of the same bawling-out Shirley had received a few minutes earlier. Finally, however, the grouchy paediatrician and I finished the task.

I reflected later on what I was feeling when Ryan was going through so much suffering. What hurt me was the look on his face. Though he was screaming and couldn't speak, he was 'talking' to me with those big blue eyes. He was saying, 'Daddy! Why are you doing this to me? I thought you loved me. I never thought you would do anything like this! How could you? Please, please! Stop hurting me!'

It was impossible to explain to Ryan that his suffering was necessary for his own good—that I was trying to help him—that it was love that required me to hold him on the table. How could I tell him of my compassion in that moment? I would gladly have taken his place on the table, if possible. But in his young mind, I was a traitor who had callously abandoned him.

Then I realised there must be times when God also feels our intense pain and suffers along with us. Wouldn't that be characteristic of a Father whose love is infinite? How He must hurt when we say in confusion, 'How could You do this terrible thing, Lord? Why me? I thought I could trust You ! I thought You were my friend!' How can He make us understand, with our human limitations, that our agony is necessary—that it *does* have a purpose—that there are answers to the tragedies of life? I wonder if He anticipates the day when He can make us understand what was occurring in our time of trial. I wonder if He broods over our sorrows.

> *There must be times when God also feels our intense pain and suffers along with us.*

Some readers might doubt that an omnipotent God with no weaknesses and no needs is vulnerable to this kind of vicarious suffering. No one can be certain. We do know that Jesus experienced the broad range of human emotions and that He told Philip, 'Anyone who has seen me has seen the Father' (John 14:9). Remember that Jesus was 'deeply moved in spirit and troubled' when Mary wept over Lazarus. He also wept as He looked over the city of

Jerusalem and spoke of the sorrow that would soon come upon the Jewish people. Likewise, we are told that the Spirit intercedes for us now with '. . . groans that words cannot express' (Romans 8:26). It seems logical to assume, therefore, that God the Father is passionately concerned about His human 'family' and shares our grief in those unspeakable moments 'when sorrows like sea billows roll'. I believe He does.

BRACE YOURSELF, AND BE PREPARED

The reason I have chosen to include this discussion in *Life on the Edge* is to help brace you, my younger readers, for those difficult times that will invade your lives sooner or later. It is inevitable. In my work with families who are going through these hardships, from sickness and death to marital conflict and financial distress, I have found it common for those in crisis to feel great frustration with God. This is particularly true when things happen that seem illogical and inconsistent with what had been taught or understood. Then if the Lord does not rescue them from the circumstances in which they are embroiled, their frustration quickly deteriorates into anger and a sense of abandonment. Finally, disillusionment sets in, and their spirits begin to wither.

This can even occur in very young children who are vulnerable to feelings of rejection from God. I'm reminded of a boy named Chris whose face had been burned in a fire. He sent this note to his psychotherapist:

Dear Dr Gardner,
Some big person, it was a boy about 13, he called me a turtle. And I know he said this because of my plastic surgery. And I think God hates me because of my lip. And when I die, he'll probably send me to hell.
Love, Chris

Chris naturally concluded that his deformity was evidence of God's rejection. It is a logical deduction in the eyes of a child: *If God is all powerful and He knows everything, then why would He let such a terrible thing happen to me? He must hate me.* Unfortunately, Chris is not alone. Many others come to believe the same satanic lie. In fact, the majority of us will someday, at some time feel a similar alienation from God. Why? Because those who live long enough will eventually be confronted by happenings they will not understand. That is the human condition.

The great danger for people who have experienced this kind of disillusionment is that Satan will use their pain to make them feel victimised by God. What a deadly trap that is! When a person begins to conclude that they are disliked or hated by the Almighty, demoralisation is not far behind.

TRIALS ARE NOTHING NEW

If you have begun to slide into that kind of despair, it is extremely important to take a new look at Scripture and recognise that you are not unique in the trials you face. All of the biblical writers, including the giants of the faith, went through similar hardships. Look at the experience of Joseph, one of the patriarchs of the Old Testament. His entire life was in shambles. He was hated by his brothers who considered killing him before agreeing instead to sell him as a slave. While in Egypt, he was imprisoned, falsely accused by Potiphar's wife of attempted rape, and threatened with execution. There is no indication that God explained to Joseph what He was doing through those many years of heartache or how the pieces would eventually fit together. He had no way of knowing that he would

> *Those who live long enough will eventually be confronted by happenings they will not understand.*

eventually enjoy a triumphal reunion with his family. He was expec-ted, as you and I are, to live out his life one day at a time in something less than complete understanding. What pleased God was Joseph's faithfulness when nothing made sense.

Let's move over to the New Testament and look at the disciples and other early Christian leaders. Jesus said there was no greater man born of woman than John the Baptist, but this honoured Christian pioneer soon found himself in Herod's stinking dungeon. There an evil woman named Herodias had him beheaded because he had condemned her immoral conduct. There is no record in Scripture that an angel visited John's cell to explain the meaning of his per-secution. This great, godly man who was the designated forerunner to Jesus went through the same confusing ex-periences as we. It is comforting to know that John res-ponded in a very human way. He sent a secret message to Jesus from his prison cell, asking, 'Are you the one who was to come, or should we expect someone else?'(Matthew. 11:2). Have you ever felt like asking that question?

Look at the the martyrdom of Stephen, who was stoned to death for proclaiming the name of Christ, and the dis-ciple James, of whom the twelfth chapter of Acts devotes only one verse: 'He [King Herod Agrippa] had James, the brother of John, put to death with a sword' (Acts 12:2). Tradition tells us that ten of the twelve disciples were even-tually executed (excluding Judas, who committed suicide, and John, who was exiled). We also believe that Paul, who was persecuted, stoned, and flogged, was later beheaded in a Roman prison. The second half of the eleventh chapter of Hebrews describes some of those who suffered for the name of Christ:

. . . Others were tortured and refused to be released, so that

they might gain a better resurrection. Some faced jeers and
flogging, while still others were chained and put in prison.
They were stoned; they were sawn in two; they were put to
death by the sword. They went about in sheepskins and
goatskins, destitute, persecuted and mistreated—the world is
not worthy of them. They wandered in deserts and mountains
and in caves and holes in the ground. These were all com-
mended for their faith, yet none of them received what had
been promised. (vv. 35–39)

Read that last verse again. Note that these saints lived in
anticipation of a promise that had not
While we are on
earth, we may never
see the purpose of
our sufferings.
been fulfilled by the time of their
deaths. A full explanation never came.
They had only their faith to hold
them steady in their time of persecu-
tion. The *Life Application Bible* commentary says of this
chapter:

These verses summarise the lives of other great men and
women of faith. Some experienced outstanding victories, even
over the threat of death. But others were severely mistreated,
tortured, and even killed. Having a steadfast faith in God does
not guarantee a happy, carefree life. On the contrary, our faith
almost guarantees us some form of abuse from the world.
While we are on earth, we may never see the purpose of our
suffering. But we know that God will keep his promises to us.

That is precisely the point.
Few of us are called upon to lay down our lives like those
heroes of the early church, but modern-day examples do
exist. Reverend Bill Hybels shared an experience in his book
Too Busy Not To Pray, that speaks dramatically to this issue:

A couple of years ago, a member of my church's vocal team

and I were invited by a Christian leader named Yesu to go to southern India. There we joined a team of people from various parts of the US. We were told that God would use us to reach Muslims and Hindus and nonreligious people for Christ. We all felt called by God to go, but none of us knew what to expect.

When we arrived, Yesu met us and invited us to his home. Over the course of the next few days, he told us about his ministry.

Yesu's father, a dynamic leader and speaker, had started the mission in a Hindu-dominated area. One day a Hindu leader came to Yesu's father and asked for prayer. Eager to pray with him, hoping he would lead him to Christ, he took him into a private room, knelt down with him, closed his eyes and began to pray. While he was praying, the Hindu man reached into his robe, pulled out a knife and stabbed him repeatedly.

Yesu, hearing his father's screams, ran to help him. He held him in his arms as blood poured out onto the floor of the hut. Three days later, his father died. On his deathbed he said to his son, 'Please tell that man that he is forgiven. Care for your mother and carry on this ministry. Do whatever it takes to win people to Christ.'

What an inspiring and humbling story! It makes me feel ashamed for complaining about the petty problems and frustrations I have encountered through the years. Someday, the Lord may require a similar sacrifice of me in the cause of Christ. If so, I pray I will have the courage to accept *whatever* His will is for me. Untold multitudes have dedicated their lives to His service in this manner.

> *Where did we get the notion that the Christian life is a piece of cake?*

So tell me, where did we get the notion that the Christian life is a piece of cake? Where is the evidence for the 'name it, claim it' theology that promises God will skip along in front of us with His great cosmic broom, sweeping aside each trial and every troubling uncertainty? To the contrary, Jesus told His disciples that they should anticipate suffering. He said, 'I have told you these things, so that in me you may have peace. In this world you will have trouble. But take heart! I have overcome the world' (John 16:33). Paul wrote, '. . . In all our troubles my joy knows no bounds. For when we came into Macedonia, this body of ours had no rest, but we were harassed at every turn—conflicts on the outside, fears within' (2 Corinthians 7:4–5). Peter left no doubt about difficulties in this Christian life when he wrote, 'Dear friends, do not be surprised at the painful trial you are suffering, as though something strange were happening to you. But rejoice that you participate in the sufferings of Christ, so that you may be overjoyed when his glory is revealed' (1 Peter 4:12–13). Note in each of these references the co-existence of both joy and pain.

This is the consistent, unequivocal expectation we have been given by the biblical writers, and yet we seem determined to rewrite the text. That makes us sitting ducks for satanic mischief.

My concern is that many believers apparently feel God owes them smooth sailing or at least a full explanation (and perhaps an apology) for the hardships they encounter. We must never forget that He, after all, is *God*. He is majestic and holy and sovereign. He is accountable to no one. He is not an errand boy who chases the assignments we dole out. He is not a genie who pops out of the bottle to satisfy our whims. He is not our servant—we are His. And our reason for existence is to glorify and honour Him.

Even so, sometimes He performs mighty miracles on our behalf. Sometimes He chooses to explain His actions in our lives. Sometimes His presence is as real as if we had encountered Him face to face. But at other times when nothing makes sense—when what we are going through is 'not fair'—when we feel all alone in God's waiting room—He simply says, 'Trust Me!'

Does this mean we are destined to be depressed and victimised by the circumstances of our lives? Certainly not. Paul said we are: 'more than conquerors'. He wrote in Philippians 4:4–7:

> Rejoice in the Lord always. I will say it again: Rejoice! Let your gentleness be evident to all. The Lord is near. Do not be anxious about anything, but in everything, by prayer and petition, with thanksgiving, present your requests to God. And the peace of God, which transcends all understanding, will guard your hearts and minds in Christ Jesus.

Clearly, what we have in Scripture is a paradox. On the one hand we are told to expect suffering and hardship that could even cost us our lives. On the other hand, we are encouraged to be joyful, thankful, and 'of good cheer'. How do those contradictory ideas link together? How can we be triumphant and under intense pressure at the same time? How can we be secure when surrounded by insecurity? That is a mystery, which, according to Paul, 'transcends all understanding'.

Clearly, what we have in Scripture is a paradox.

For those of you out there today who have already been through hard times and are desperate for a word of encouragement, let me assure you that you *can* trust this Lord of heaven and earth. Remember that Scripture warns us to '. . . lean not on your own understanding' (Proverbs 3:5).

Note that we are not prohibited from trying to understand. I've spent a lifetime attempting to get a grip on some of the imponderables of life. But we are specifically told not to *lean* on our ability to make the pieces fit. 'Leaning' refers to the panicky demand for answers—throwing faith to the wind if a satisfactory response cannot be produced. It is pressing God to explain Himself—or else! That is where everything starts to unravel.

If we can comprehend even a tiny portion of the Lord's majesty and the depth of His love for us, we can deal with those times when He defies human logic and sensibilities. Indeed, that is what we *must* do. Expect confusing experiences to occur along the way, and don't be dismayed when they arrive. Welcome them as friends—as opportunities for your faith to grow. Hold fast to your faith, without which it is impossible to please Him. 'Lean into the pain' when your time to suffer comes around. Never yield to feelings of self-pity or victimisation, which are Satan's most effective tools against us. Instead, store away your questions for a lengthy conversation in eternity, and then press on towards the mark. Any other approach is foolhardy.

> *Let me assure you that you can trust this Lord of heaven and earth.*

16

ANSWERING THE ETERNAL QUESTIONS

One of my professional colleagues died towards the end of my final year on the staff of Children's Hospital of Los Angeles. He had served on our university medical faculty for more than twenty-five years. During his tenure as a professor, he had earned the respect and admiration of both professionals and patients, especially for his research findings and contribution to medical knowledge. This doctor had reached the pinnacle of success in his chosen field and enjoyed the status and financial rewards that accompany such accomplishment. He had tasted every good thing, at least by the standards of the world.

At the next staff meeting following his death, a five-minute eulogy was read by a member of his department. Then the chairman invited the entire staff to stand, as is our custom in situations of this nature, for one minute of silence in memory of our fallen colleague. I have no idea what the other members of the staff thought about during that sixty-second pause, but I can tell you what was going through my mind.

I was thinking, *Lord, is this what it all comes down to? We sweat and worry and labour to achieve a place in life, to impress our fellow men with our competence. We take ourselves so seriously, over-reacting to the insignificant events of each passing day. Then finally, even for the brightest among us, all these successes fade into history and our lives are summarised with a five-minute eulogy and sixty seconds of silence. It hardly seems worth the effort, Lord.*

But I was also struck by the collective inadequacy of that faculty to deal with the questions raised by our friend's death. Where had he gone? Would he live again? Will we see him on the other side? Why was he born? Were his deeds observed and recorded by a loving God? Is that God interested in me? Is there a purpose to life beyond investigative research and professorships and expensive automobiles? The silent response by 250 learned men and women seemed to symbolise our inability to cope with these issues.

Well, how about it? Do you know where you stand on the fundamental issues posed by the death of my friend? More to the point, have you resolved them for yourself and for those you love? If not, then I hope you'll read on. We will devote this final chapter to those questions and to the search for life's ultimate meaning and purpose.

It is a matter of incredible significance. Until we know who we are and why we are here, no amount of success, fame, money, or pleasure will provide much satisfaction. Until we get a fix on the 'big picture', nothing will make much sense.

As I indicated in an earlier chapter, it is so important to pause and think through some of these basic issues while you are young, before the pressures of job and family become distracting. Everyone must deal with the eternal questions sooner or later. You will benefit, I think, from doing that work now. As I said earlier, whether you are an atheist, a Muslim, a Buddhist, a Jew, a New-Ager, an agnostic, or a Christian, the questions confronting the human family are the same. Only the answers will differ.

LIFE: WHAT'S IT ALL ABOUT?

Millions of people acknowledge today that they do not know the meaning of life. Indeed, sociologists tell us that a desperate search for spiritual truth is underway throughout Western cultures. Baby boomers have been seeking something to believe in for almost three decades. In the 1970s, they were involved in a quest that came to be known as 'the discov-

Until we get a fix on the 'big picture', nothing will make much sense.

ery of personhood'. It motivated some of them to participate in nude counselling, transcendental meditation, reincarnation and other Eastern mysticism, ESP, astrology, psychoanalysis, therapeutic massage, far-out theologies, and a seminar on the self called EST (Erhard Seminar Training).

The quest for personhood failed miserably. Indeed, most people came out of these programmes more confused and frustrated than before. They looked for the answers to life's questions within themselves and were inevitably disappointed. Here's why.

When I was four years old, I was digging in the yard and discovered a bed of onions my aunt had planted that spring. Not knowing what they were, I began trying to peel them. As I tore away the outer layer, I found another shiny one tucked underneath. When that one was stripped away, yet another lay below. The onion just got smaller and smaller as I clawed at its structure. My aunt was shocked a few minutes later to find fragments of her prized onions spread all over the lawn.

Human beings are like those onions in some ways. When you strip away all the layers one by one, not much remains to 'discover'. You will never find real meaning among your selfish interests, feelings, and aspirations. The answers do not lie within you. In fact, the more you promote yourself, the emptier you feel.

Jesus addressed that precise issue when He said, 'If any man will come after me, let him deny himself, and take up his cross daily, and follow me. For whosoever will save his life shall lose it: but whosoever will lose his life for my sake, the same shall save it' (Luke 9:23–24 KJV). In other words, meaning and purpose will be found outside—not inside—the onion.

Where will you find answers to the major questions of life? How will you identify the values that moth and rust will not corrupt and thieves cannot break in and steal? All of us are faced with these questions. How can they be answered?

THE BREVITY OF LIFE

It might be useful to engage in a mental exercise I call the 'end-of-life test'. Project yourself many years down the road when your time on earth is drawing to a close. That may seem morbid to you at such a young age, but the brevity of life is a very important biblical concept. The psalmist David said our lives are like the flowers of the field that blossom in the morning and then fade away (see Psalm 103:15–16). Moses expressed the same idea in Psalm 90 when he wrote,

> *Where will you find answers to the major questions of life?*

'Teach us to number our days . . .' (v. 12 KJV). What the biblical writers were telling us is that we're just passing through. At best, we're merely short-termers on this planet.

Given this understanding of the brevity of life, I invite you to imagine yourself as an old man or woman looking back across many decades. Think about the highlights and treasures of the past seventy or eighty years. What kinds of memories will be the most precious to you in that final hour?

I may be in a position to help answer these questions because I've had to deal with them. It began on a basketball court a few years ago. At fifty-four years of age, I thought I was in great physical condition. I had recently undergone a medical examination and was pronounced to be in excellent health. I could play basketball all day with men twenty-five years my junior. But there were unpleasant surprises in store for me on that particular morning.

As I went in for a lay-up, I was seized by a pain in the centre of my chest. It was unlike anything I'd ever experienced. I excused myself, telling my friends I didn't feel well. Then I drove to a nearby emergency clinic. Incidentally, this was the same hospital where my dad was taken after suffering a massive heart attack twenty-one years earlier. So began ten days that would change my life.

What kinds of memories will be the most precious to you in that final hour?

For a man who thought of himself as 'Joe College', it was a shock to realise that I might be dying. It took awhile for that thought to sink in. But about ten hours later, an enzyme report confirmed that I had had a heart attack. Nurses came at me from every direction. Tubes and IVs were strung all over me. An automatic blood pressure machine pumped frantically on my arm throughout the night, and a supervising nurse delicately suggested that I do not move unless absolutely necessary. That does tend to get your attention.

As I lay there in the darkness listening to the beep-beep-beep of my heart on the oscilloscope, I began to think very clearly about what really mattered in my life. As I've said, encountering death has a way of jerking your priorities into line. Everything fluffy and insignificant falls away, and the true values begin to shine like burnished gold. I knew that I was ready to go if the Lord should beckon me across the

great divide. I had lived my life so as to be prepared for such
a time as that, but I didn't expect it to come so quickly.

*Encountering
death has a way
of jerking your
priorities into
line.*

Fortunately for me, the damage to my
heart proved to be minor, and God has
restored me to vigorous health. I exercise
every day, and I'm eating some of the
finest birdseed money can buy. Still, that
scary experience in the hospital made an
indelible impression on me and gave me a new zest for life.

WHEN EVERYTHING IS ON THE LINE

That's why I have a good notion of how you're likely to react
when your time in the 'white water' comes around. Ask
yourself what you will care about when everything is on the
line. Will it be the businesses you created and nourished?
Will it be the plaques that hang on the wall? Will it be the
academic degrees you earned from prestigious universities?
Will it be the fortune you accumulated? Will it be the
speeches you gave, the paintings you produced, or the songs
you sang? Will it be the books you wrote or the offices to
which you were elected? Will it be the power and influence
you held? Will it be a five-minute eulogy and sixty seconds
of silence after you're gone? I doubt it.

Achievements and the promise of posthumous acclaim
will bring some satisfaction, no doubt. But your highest
priorities will be drawn from another source. When all is
said and done and the books are closing on your life, I
believe your treasures will lie much closer to home. Your
most precious memories will focus on those you loved, those
who loved you, and what you did together in the service of
the Lord. Those are the basics. Nothing else will survive the
scrutiny of time.

To elaborate on that concept, let me take you back to that

gymnasium where my heart attack occurred. Two years earlier, another highly significant event had occurred just a few feet from where I was stricken. My friends and I played basketball three times a week on that court, and on that particular morning, we had invited Pete Maravich to join us.

It was an audacious thing to do. 'Pistol Pete', as he was dubbed by the media, had been one of the greatest basketball players of all times. He was the Michael Jordan or the Magic Johnson of his day. He set more than forty NCAA college records at Louisiana State University, many of which still stand. He had averaged forty-four points per game during his three years at LSU. After graduation, Pete was drafted by the National Basketball Association and became the first player ever to receive a million-dollar contract. When he retired because of knee problems, he was elected to the NBA Hall of Fame the first year he was eligible. There is very little that can be done with a basketball that Pete Maravich didn't accomplish.

So for a bunch of 'duffers' to invite a superstar like Pete to play with us took some gall, even though he was forty years old at the time. To our delight, he agreed to come and showed up at 7.00 a.m. I quickly learned that he had been suffering from an unidentified pain in his right shoulder for many months. Aside from playing in the NBA 'Legends Game', which was televised nationally, Pete had not been on a basketball court in more than a year. Nevertheless, we had a good time that morning. Pete moved at about one-third his normal speed, and the rest of us huffed and puffed to keep up. We played for about forty-five minutes and then took a break to get a drink. Pete and I stayed on the court and talked while waiting for the other players to come back.

'You can't give up this game, Pete,' I said. 'It has meant too much to you through the years.'

'You know, I've loved playing this morning,' he replied. 'I

really do want to get back to this kind of recreational basketball. But it wouldn't have been possible in the last few
months. The pain in my shoulder has been so intense that I
couldn't have lifted a two-pound ball over my head.'

'How are you feeling today?' I asked.

'I feel great,' he said.

PETE'S LAST WORDS

Those were Pete's last words. I turned to walk away, and for
some reason looked back in time to see him fall down. His
face and body hit the boards hard. Still, I thought he was
teasing. Pete had a great sense of humour, and I assumed
that he was playing off his final comment about feeling
good.

I hurried over to where Pete lay and still expected him to
get up laughing. But then I saw that he was having a seizure.
I held his tongue to keep his air passage open and called for
the other guys to come and help me. The seizure lasted
about twenty seconds, and then Pete stopped breathing. We
started artificial respiration immediately, but were never able
to get another heartbeat or another breath. Pistol Pete
Maravich, one of the world's greatest athletes, died there in
my arms at forty years of age.

Several of us accompanied the ambulance to the hospital,
where we prayerfully watched the emergency room staff try
to revive Pete for about forty-five minutes. But it was no
use. He had left this earth, and there was nothing anyone
could do to bring him back.

An autopsy revealed a few days later that Pete had a congenital malformation of the heart and never knew it. That
was why his shoulder had been hurting. Whereas most of us
have two coronary arterial systems that wrap around the
heart, Pete only had one. How he was able to do such

incredible exploits on the basketball court for so many years is a medical mystery. He was destined to drop dead at a fairly young age, and only God knows why it happened during the brief moment when his path crossed mine.

The shock of Pete's untimely death is impossible to describe. None of the men who witnessed the tragedy will ever forget it. My heart goes out to his lovely wife, Jackie, and their two sons, Jason and Joshua. I spoke at his funeral three days later and still feel a bond of friendship with his family.

> *Pistol Pete Maravich . . . died there in my arms at forty years of age.*

It is important to know something about Pete's background to understand who he was. Quite frankly, he had been a troublemaker when he was younger. He was a heavy drinker who broke all the rules. His attitude deteriorated in the NBA, and he finally resigned in a huff. This man who had received every acclaim that can come to an athlete hit rock bottom emotionally. After retirement, he stayed in his house day after day to avoid autograph-seeking fans and because he had nowhere to go. There he sat, depressed and angry, for two years.

Something incredible happened at that crucial moment in Pete's life. He was in bed one night when he heard someone speak his name. He sat upright, wondering if he had been dreaming. Then he heard the voice again. Pete realised that God was calling him. He immediately knelt beside his bed and gave his heart to the Lord. It was a total consecration of his mind, body, and soul.

For the last five years of his life, all he wanted to talk about was what Jesus Christ had done for him. He told that story to reporters, to coaches, to fans, and to anyone who would listen. The day Pete died, he was wearing a T-shirt that bore the inscription, 'Looking unto Jesus'.

I was able to share that testimony with the media, which took it around the world within an hour. 'You think Pete's great love was basketball,' I told them, 'but that was not his passion. All he really cared about was Jesus Christ and what He had done in Pete's life.' And now I'm relaying that message to you. Perhaps that is why the Lord placed this good man in my arms as his life ebbed away.

HITTING CLOSE TO HOME

Now I need to tell you something highly personal that happened next. I went home and sat down with our son, Ryan, who was seventeen years old at the time. I asked to talk to him about something of extreme importance to us both.

I said, 'Ryan, I want you to understand what has happened here. Pete's death was not an unusual tragedy that has happened to only one man and his family. We all must face death sooner or later and in one way or another. This is the 'human condition'. It comes too early for some people and too late for others. But no one will escape, ultimately. And, of course, it will also happen to you and me. So without being morbid about it, I want you to begin to prepare yourself for that time.

'Sooner or later, you'll get the kind of phone call that Mrs Maravich received. It could occur ten or fifteen years from now, or it could come tomorrow. But when that time comes, there is one thought I want to leave with you. I don't know if I'll have an opportunity to give you my "last words" then, so let me express them to you right now. Freeze-frame this moment in your mind, and hold on to it for the rest of your life. My message to you is *Be there!* Be there to meet your mother and me in heaven. We will be looking for you on that resurrection morning. Don't let anything deter you from keeping that appointment.

'Because I am fifty-one years old and you are only seventeen, as many as fifty years could pass from the time of my death to yours. That's a long time to remember. But you can be sure that I will be searching for you just inside the Eastern Gate. This is the only thing of real significance in your life. I care what you accomplish in the years to come, and I hope you make good use of the great potential the Lord has given to you. But above every other purpose and goal, the only thing that really matters is that you determine now to *be there!*'

That message is not only the most valuable legacy I could leave to Ryan and his sister, Danae. It is also the heart and soul of what I have tried to convey in this book. *Be there!* This must be our ultimate objective in living. Within that two-word phrase are answers to all the other questions we have posed.

Jesus Christ is the source—the *only* source—of meaning in life. He provides the only satisfactory explanation for why we're here and where we're going. Because of

> *My message to you is*
> **Be there!**

this good news, the final heartbeat for the Christian is not the mysterious conclusion to a meaningless existence. It is, rather, the grand beginning to a life that will never end.

That same Lord is waiting to embrace and forgive anyone who comes to Him in humility and repentance. He is calling your name, just as He called the name of Pete Maravich. His promise of eternal life offers the only hope for humanity. If you have never met this Jesus, I suggest that you seek spiritual counsel from a Christian leader who can offer guidance. You can also write to me, if that would help.

Thanks for reading along with me. I hope to meet you someday. If our paths don't cross this side of heaven, I'll be looking for you in that eternal city. By all means, *Be there!*

ADDENDUM

THIRTY-EIGHT VALUES TO LIVE BY

Listed below are thirty-eight principles I have drawn on from a lifetime of experience in Christian living and in human interaction. I believe you will find them workable in your own lives. Many of these items are drawn from the text you have just read. They are listed here to serve as a summary of the concepts we've discussed.

1.   'Seek ye first the kingdom of God, and his righteousness; and all these things shall be added unto you' (Matthew 6:33 KJV). This is the fundamental principle of life on which all others rest.

2.   Overcommitment and time pressure are the greatest destroyers of marriages and families. It takes *time* to develop any friendship . . . whether with a loved one or with God Himself.

3.   The overwhelming feeling of being 'in love' is not a very reliable emotion during the early years (or at any age!). This intense affection can evaporate in a matter of days, leaving the person confused (and perhaps unhappily married). The only way to know you are in love with another person is to give yourselves plenty of time to get acquainted. Once the decision is made to marry, then your *commitment*

to one another will be much more important than your feelings, which are certain to come and go.

4.   The universe and everything in it will someday pass away and be made new by the Creator. Therefore, the events of *today* that seem so important are not really very significant, except those matters that will survive the end of the universe (such as securing your own salvation and doing the work of the Lord).

5.   God is like a father to His children. He loves them more than they can understand, but He also expects them to be obedient to His will. And He has said, 'The wages of sin is death' (Rom. 6:23 KJV). It is still true.

6.   This is the way to be successful in life: Treat every person as you want to be treated; look for ways to meet the physical, emotional and spiritual needs of those around you. Suppress your desire to be selfish and to seek unfair advantage over others. Try to turn *every* encounter with another person into a new or stronger friendship. Then when this confidence with people is combined with hard work, your future success is assured.

7.   Human worth does not depend on beauty, intelligence, or accomplishments. We are all more valuable than the possessions of the entire world simply because God gave us that value. This fact remains true, even if every other person on earth treats us like losers.

8.   Strong desire is like a river. As long as it flows within the banks of God's will—be the current strong or weak—all is well. But when it overruns those boundaries and seeks its own channels, then disaster lurks in the rampage below— *James Dobson Sr.*

9.   The killing of unborn children through medical

abortions is one of the most evil occurrences of our time, with 1.5 million babies sacrificed in America and 55 million worldwide each year.

10.   Comparison is the root of all feelings of inferiority. The moment you begin examining other people's strengths against your most obvious weaknesses, your self-esteem starts to crumble!

11.   As a general rule, don't risk what you can't afford to lose.

12.   There will come a day, much quicker than your parents would wish, when you will no longer be comfortable living at home. You will want to move out and establish a home of your own. After that time, your mother and father will be more like your friends than your parents. And someday, if they live long enough, you will be more like a parent to them than a son or daughter.

13.   If you're going through difficult times, hold steady. It will change soon. If you are experiencing smooth sailing and easy times now, brace yourself. It will change soon. The only thing you can be certain of is change.

14.   God created *two* sexes, male and female. They are equal in worth, although each is unique and different. It is not only impossible to blend maleness and femaleness into a single sex (unisex), it is dangerous to even attempt it.

15.   'The *love* of money is the root of all evil '(1 Timothy 6:10 KJV). That's why Jesus issues more warnings about materialism and wealth than any other sin. Obviously, it takes a steady hand to hold a full cup.

16.   Christians should never consult astrologers, psychics or those who practise witchcraft (see Isaiah 47:13–14).

They are usually phonies who only pretend to have extrasensory powers. But in some cases, they are working in cooperation with Satan. Rather than tamper with this evil world, the one true God wants us to bring our needs, problems, and decisions to Him. He has promised to lead us into all truth (see John 8:32).

17.   One of the secrets of successful living is found in the word *balance,* referring to the avoidance of harmful extremes. We need food, but we should not overeat. We should work, but not make work our only activity. We should play, but not let play rule us. Throughout life, it will be important to find the safety of the middle ground rather than the imbalance of the extremes.

18.   Your life is before you. Be careful of the choices you make now that you could regret later. This regret is the subject of an old poem whose author has been forgotten. I hope you'll never have reason to apply it to yourself.

> Across the fields of yesterday,
> He sometimes comes to me
> A little lad just back from play—
> The boy I used to be.
> He looks at me so wistfully
> When once he's crept within;
> It is as if he hoped to see
> The man I might have been.

19.   Those who are the happiest are not necessarily those for whom life has been easiest. Emotional stability results from an attitude. It is refusing to yield to depression and fear, even when black clouds float overhead. It is improving that which can be improved and accepting that which is inevitable.

20.   Communism and socialism are economic systems whereby the government assumes responsibility to see that each person's needs are met and that no one individual earns more than the state feels is fair. Capitalism, such as we have in America, is based on free enterprise, whereby a person can achieve a better income for himself and his family by working and sweating and saving and investing. To compare these systems, think of yourself about to take a history test. Suppose you studied very hard and earned an A, but the teacher gave you a C so he could share some of your correct answers with a failing student who didn't study at all. Obviously this would destroy your motivation to study in the future. This need for personal incentives explains why capitalism produces more energetic people than communism and socialism, and why America is the richest nation on earth.

21.   Take in a great breath of air and then blow it out. Contained in that single breath were at least three nitrogen atoms that were breathed by every human being who ever lived, including Jesus Christ, William Shakespeare, Winston Churchill, and every president of the United States. This illustrates the fact that everything we do affects other people, positively or negatively. That's why it is foolish to say, 'Do your own thing if it doesn't hurt anybody else.' Everything we do affects other people.

22.   Faith in God is like believing a man can walk over Niagara Falls on a tightrope while pushing a wheelbarrow. Trust in God is like getting in the wheelbarrow! To believe God can do something miraculous is one thing; to risk His willingness to do it in your life is another.

23.   With God, even when nothing is happening . . . something is happening.

24.   The first five minutes of everything are virtually important, especially to:

A new friendship,
A pastor's sermon,
A family during the early-morning hours,
A dad who has just come home from work,
A television programme,
A salesman's presentation,
A visit to the doctor.

Those first few moments of any human activity set the stage for everything that follows. If we begin our task properly, we will probably be successful over the long haul. Therefore, spend more time preparing for the first five minutes than any comparable period of time.

25.   Whenever two human beings spend time together, sooner or later they will probably irritate one another. This is true of best friends, married couples, parents and children, or teachers and students. The question is: How do they respond when friction occurs? There are four basic ways they can react:

*   They can internalise the anger and send it downwards into a memory bank that never forgets. This creates great pressure within and can even result in disease and other problems.

*   They can pout and be rude without discussing the issues. This further irritates the other person and leaves them to draw their own conclusions about what the problem may be.

*   They can blow-up and try to hurt the other person. This causes the death of friendships, marriages, homes, and businesses.

* Or they can talk to one another about their feelings, being very careful not to attack the dignity and worth of the other person. This approach often leads to permanent and healthy relationships.

26. Don't marry someone with intolerable characteristics in the hope of changing them. If you can't live with someone who drinks or someone who isn't a Christian or someone who isn't clean, then don't marry that kind of person. The chances for miraculous improvement or changes in behaviour are slim. What you see is what you get!

27. 'Except the Lord build a house, they labour in vain that build it' (Psalm 127:1 KJV).

28. Feelings are neither right nor wrong. It's what you do with them that causes the problems.

29. Most loneliness results from insulation rather than isolation. In other words, we are lonely because we insulate ourselves, not because others isolate us.

30. Some men watch so many sporting events on television that they wouldn't even know of their wives' decision to divorce them unless it was announced on 'Monday Night Football'! Remember, balance and moderation are needed in television watching, too.

31. The human body seems indestructible when we are young. However, it is incredibly fragile and must be cared for if it is to serve us for a lifetime. Too often, the abuse it takes during early years (from drugs, improper nutrition, sporting injuries, etc.) become painful handicaps during later years.

32. Before you criticise your parents for their failures and mistakes, ask yourself: 'Will I really do that much better

with my own children?' The job is tougher than it looks, and mistakes are inevitable!

33.   Satan will attempt to offer you whatever you hunger for, whether it be money, power, sex, or prestige. But Jesus said, 'Blessed are those who hunger and thirst for righteousness' (Matthew 5:6).

34.   Sexual contact between a boy and a girl is a progressive thing. In other words, the amount of touching and caressing and kissing that occurs in the early days tends to increase as they become more familiar and at ease with one another. Likewise, the amount of contact necessary to excite one another increases day by day, leading in many cases to an ultimate act of sin and its inevitable consequence. This progression must be consciously resisted by young Christian people who want to serve God and live by His standards. They can resist this trend by placing deliberate controls on the physical aspect of their relationship, right from the first date.

35.   God is entitled to a portion of our income—not because He needs it but because we need to give it.

36.   'For what shall it profit a man if he shall gain the whole world, and lose his own soul?' (Jesus' words in Mark 8:36 KJV).

37.   It is better to be single and unhappy than unhappily married.

38.   'A wet bird never flies at night'. (My grandfather said that to me when I was a child and warned me not to forget it. I remember his words but never did figure out what he meant!)

NOTES

Chapter 1 — *Blast Off or Blow Up?*
1. Katherine Seligman, 'More Children Than Cops Are Shot in the US', *San Francisco Examiner*, 21 January 1994, A16.

Chapter 2 — *The Courtroom of the Mind*
1. Cartoon courtesy of Dr Brian Moench and In Your Face Cards.
2. Laurel Mellini, University of California at San Francisco, 1986.

Chapter 3 — *For Love of Money*
1. 'Eleanor Rigby', The Beatles, © 1966 Capitol Records, MacLen Music—EMI/Blackwood (ASCAP).
2. Ron and Judy Blue, *Money Matters for Parents and Their Kids* (Nashville: Thomas Nelson, 1988), 46.

Chapter 4 — *The Powerbrokers*
1. Brendan C. Boyd and Fred C. Harris, *The Great American Baseball Card Flipping, Trading, and Bubble Gum Book*, 1991.
2. *Hollywood*, 'Episode 12: Star Treatment', Thames Television Network, London, England, 1980.

Chapter 5 — *Questions from the Edge*
1. 'Day Care Diseases: Exploring the Risks of Centre-Based Care', Family Research Council, May/June 1989.
2. Stella Chess, MD, and Alexander Thomas, MD, *Know Your Child: An Authoritative Guide for Today's Parents* (New York: Basic Books, 1987), 123–4.

Chapter 6 — *The Keys to Lifelong Love*
1. US Bureau of the Census, *Statistical Abstract of the United States: 1993*, 113th edition, Washington, DC, 1993.
2. Helen Richards, 'God's Protection During War and Peace', *Focus*

on the Family Magazine, 20–22 July, 1987.

3. Armand Nicholi, MD, 'Changes in the American Family', Family Research Council, 1986.

4. Reprinted by permission from *American Girl,* a magazine for girls, published by the Girl Scouts, USA.

5. Desmond Morris, *Intimate Behaviour* (New York: Random House, 1971).

6. 'All the Way', Frank Sinatra, © 1957, Capitol Records.

7. Don Reid and Harold Heid, 'The Official Historian on Shirley Jane Burrell', recorded by the Statler Brothers, American Cowboy Music Company, All Nations Music Publishing, Ltd./Music of the World (BMI), 8857 W. Olympic Blvd., Suite 200, Beverly Hills, CA 90211. Used by permission.

8. Tina Turner, 'What's Love Got to Do with It?' © 1984, Capitol Records.

9. Larry L. Bumpass, James A. Sweet, and Andrew Cherlin, 'The Role of Cohabitation in Declining Rates of Marriage', *Journal of Marriage and the Family* 53 (1991): 913–27.

Chapter 7 — Love Must Be Tough

1. Jack London, 'To Build a Fire', from *To Build a Fire and Other Short Stories* (Mankato, Minn.: Creative Education).

2. Betty Cuniberti, 'Man Spends $20,000 Trying to Win Hand of Girl Who Can Say No', *Los Angeles Times.* Reprinted by permission.

3. Virginia Doody Klein, 'Living with Divorce', a syndicated column published in the *Los Angeles Times, 12 April 1982,* © *1982 Sun Features, Inc.* Used by permission.

4. Tom T. Hall, 'I Left You Some Kisses on the Door', © 1979 Hallnote Music. Used by permission.

Chapter 8 — Questions from the Edge

1. Keith and Mary Korstjens, 'Not a Sometimes Love', *Focus on the Family Magazine,* 14 February 1983.

2. Carly Simon and Jacob Brackman, 'That's the Way I've Always Heard it Should Be', © Warner Brothers Music, Inc. All rights reserved. Used by permission.

3. US Bureau of the Census, *Statistical Abstract of the United States: 1993,* 113th edition, Washington, DC, 53.

4. Stella Chess, MD, and Alexander Thomas, MD, *Know Your Child,* 33.

Chapter 9 — Getting Along with Your Parents
1. Eddie Fisher, 'Oh, My Papa', © 1953 RCA-Victor Records, English words by John Turner and Geoffrey Parsons; music and original lyric by Paul Burkhard; copyright © 1948, 1950 Musikverlag und Buhnenvertrieb Zurich A.G., Zurich, Switzerland; copyright © 1953 Shapiro, Bernstein, & Co., Inc., New York. Copyrights renewed. International copyright secured. All rights reserved. Used by permission.
2. The Doors, 'The End', © 1968 Viva Records.
3. The Coasters, 'Yakkety-Yak (Don't Talk Back), © 1953 Atco Records.
4. Twisted Sister, 'We're Not Gonna Take It', © 1984 Atlantic Records.
5. Suicidal Tendencies, 'I Saw Your Mummy', written by Michael Muir, © 1984 You'll Be Sorry Music (BMI)/American Lesion Music (BMI)/Administered by BUG. All Rights reserved. Used by permission.
6. Ice-T and Body Count, 'Mumma's Gonna Die Tonight', © 1992 Sire Records.
7. Jill Brookes, 'Its Empire Stretches Worldwide', *New York Post,* 22 April 1993, 21.
8. Erma Bombeck, *If Life is a Bowl of Cherries, What Am I Doing in the Pits?* (New York: Random-Fawcett, 1979).
9. Sue Kidd, 'Don't Let it End This Way', *Focus on the Family Magazine,* January 1985, 6–7, 11.
10. International Catholic Bureau, Lusanne, Switzerland, 24 March 1994, 15.

Chapter 10 — Emotions: Friend or Foe?
1. 'Alabama Incident is Classic Case of Hysteria', *Medical Tribune,* 19 September 1973, 1, 7.

Chapter 11 — The Hallway of Doors
1. N. M. Malamuth, M. Heim, and S. Feshbach, *Journal of Personality and Social Psychology* (1980): 38, 399–408.

Chapter 12 — Further down the Hallway
1. Adolescent enrolment in only one federal program=Title X=from 1970=92 totals more than one billion dollars.
2. Pamela McConnell, Sexually Transmitted Diseases Division, Centres for Disease Control, t.i. 16 March 1992.
3. Stephen Genuis, M.D., 'The Dilemma of Adolescent Sexuality:

'Part 1: The Onslaught of Sexually Transmitted Diseases', *Journal of SOGC* 15, no. 5 (June/July 1993): 556.

4. *1991 Division of STD/HIV Prevention. Annual Report,* US Department of Health and Human Services, Public Health Service, Centres for Disease Control, 13.

5. Ibid.

6. Felicity Barringer, 'Viral Sexual Diseases are Found in One in Five in the US', *New York Times,* 1 April 1993, A1.

7. *1991 Division of STD/HIV Prevention Annual Report,* 13.

8. 'Barbara Reed MD, MSPH, et al, 'Factors Associated with Human Papilloma Virus Infection in Women Encountered in Community-Based Offices', *Archive of Family Medicine, 290,* 2 (December 1993): 1,239.

9. Ibid.

10. Heidi M. Bauer, 'Genital HPV Infection in Female University Students as Determined by a PCR-Based Method', *Journal of the American Medical Association* 265, no. 472 (1991).

11. Elise F. Jones and Josephine Dorroch Forrest, 'Contraceptive Failure in the United States: Revised Estimates from the 1982 National Survey of Family Growth', *Family Planning Perspectives* 21 (May/June 1989): 103.

12. Susan C. Weller, 'A Meta-Analysis of Condom Effectiveness in Reducing Sexually Transmitted HIV', *Social Science and Medicine* 35, no. 36 (June 1993): 1,635–44.

13. Dr Kenneth Noeller, *OB/GYN Clinical Alert,* September 1992.

14. *UTMB News,* University of Texas Medical Branch at Galveston, 7 June 1993, citing a press release related to Susan C. Weller, 'A Meta-Analysis of Condom Effectiveness in Reducing Sexually Transmitted HIV', *Social Science and Medicine.*

15. Theresa Crenshaw, remarks made at the National Conference on HIV, Washington, DC, 15–18 November 1991.

16. Barringer, 'Viral Sexual Diseases are Found in One in Five in the US'.

Chapter 13 — Questions from the Edge

1. Doug Scott, *Inside Planned Parenthood* (Grand Rapids: Frontlines, 1990), 78.

2. Felicity Barringer, 'Viral Sexual Diseases are Found in One in Five in the US'.

3. Richard D. Glascow, Ph.D, 'The Most Commonly Asked Questions about RU-486', *National Right to Life News,* 28 April 1993, 12–13.

4. *The Alan Guttmacher Institute 1994 Report: Sex and America's Teenagers* (New York: 1994), 28.
5. Adelle Banks, 'Some Kids Agree in Survey: Rape OK if Date Costs Money', *Los Angeles Herald-Examiner*, 8 May 1988, A14.

Chapter 14 — Choosing a College

1. Dinesh D'Souza, 'The Visigoths in Tweed', *Forbes*, 1 April 1992, 82.
2. Todd Ackerman, 'Decision Could Kill College Speech Codes', *Houston Chronicle*, 28 June 1993, A1.
3. John Leo, 'The Academy's New Ayatollahs', *US News and World Report*, 10 December 1990, 22.
4. Carol Innerst, ' "Sensitivity" is the Buzzword at Colleges', *Washington Times*, 29 August 1990, A1.
5. Leo, 'New Ayatollahs', 22.
6. Edward Lucas, 'Free Speech Falls to the Campus Thought Police: The Fight Against Racism and Sexism is Creating Another Oppression', *The Independent*, 9 June 1991, 13.
7. Stephen Chapman, 'Campus Speech Codes are on the Way to Extinction', *Chicago Tribune*, 9 July 1992, 21.
8. Barbara Vobejda, 'Shalala: A Lifetime Spent in the Centre of the Storms: Tough Questions Likely for HHS Designee', *Washington Post*, 20 December 1992, A13.
9. Dennis Kelly, 'A Call for a Return to Liberal Arts Education', *USA Today*, 4 March 1993, 4D.
10. William Celis, 'College Curriculums Shaken to the Core', *New York Times*, 10 January 1993, 4A.
11. Ibid.
12. Bob Greene, 'What Does the Naked Guy Tell us about Our Society?' *Dallas Morning News*, 14 February 1993, 7J.
13. Hilary Appelman, 'Cornell University President Considering Gay Living Unit Proposal', Associated Press, 24 March 1993.
14. Ibid.
15. Scott W. Wright, '1 in 100 Tested at UT Has AIDS Virus', *Austin American-Statesman*, 14 July 1991, A14.
16. Robin Wilson, 'Sexually Active Students Playing Russian Roulette', *Seattle Times*, 6 February 1992, A9.
17. David Gates, 'White Male Paranoia', *Newsweek*, 29 March 1993, 28–54.
18. Abraham Lincoln, 'Government Cannot Endure Half-Slave and Half-Free', Republican State Convention, Springfield, Illinois, 16 June 1858. See also Matthew 12:25.

DR JAMES DOBSON is founder and president of Focus on the Family, a non-profit evangelical organisation dedicated to the preservation of the home. He is recognised as one of America's foremost authorities on the family and is the author of numerous books, including *The New Dare to Discipline, The Strong-Willed Child, When God Doesn't Make Sense, Love Must Be Tough, Straight Talk,* and *Parenting isn't for Cowards,* as well as the video series that accompanies this book, *Life on the Edge.* Dr Dobson is a licensed Marriage, Family and Child Therapist in the State of Colorado. He was formerly an assistant professor of paediatrics at the University of Southern California, School of Medicine. His international radio broadcast, 'Focus on the Family', is heard on more than two thousand stations worldwide. He and his wife, Shirley, are the parents of two young adult children, Ryan and Danae.

OTHER BOOKS BY DR JAMES DOBSON

Hide or Seek
Dare to Discipline
Love Must Be Tough
The Strong-Willed Child
Parenting isn't for Cowards
Emotions: Can You Trust Them?
Dr Dobson Answers Your Questions
When God Doesn't Make Sense
Straight Talk to Men and Their Wives
Children at Risk (with Gary L. Bauer)
Preparing for Adolescence
Love for a Lifetime
What Wives Wish Their Husbands Knew about Women